The New Economics
of
Sustainable Development

A Briefing for Policy Makers

THE NEW ECONOMICS OF SUSTAINABLE DEVELOPMENT

A Briefing for Policy Makers

James Robertson

Foreword by Jean-Claude Thébault

Office for Official Publications of the European Communities

KOGAN PAGE

British Library Cataloguing in Publication Data
A CIP record for this book is available from the British Library

First published in 1999

© European Communities, 1999

Office for Official Publications of the European Communities
2 rue Mercier, L–2985 Luxembourg
ISBN 92-828-7456-7
Catalogue No CM-23-99-677-EN-C

Kogan Page
120 Pentonville Road, London N1 9JN
kpinfo@kogan-page.co.uk
www.kogan-page.co.uk

ISBN 0 7494 3093 1

Typeset by JS Typesetting, Wellingborough, Northants
Printed in Great Britain by Biddles Ltd, Guildford and King's Lynn

Contents

Foreword

The challenging of truths still recently considered to be universal has swept through the world of pure science and now of economics. Ever since the Club of Rome sounded the alarm, the clash between the accepted truths of classical economics and the new ideas launched by the current of sustainable development has challenged a number of certainties and beliefs solidly anchored in our system of thought.

In a changing world, this new current of thought has the advantage of offering new avenues for decision-makers to explore and of generating debate on what sustainable development should be. Now that the Euro is on the verge of becoming reality, the European Union is more than ever affected by the need to offer citizens a kind of development which can meet the needs of the present, but without compromising the capacity of future generations to meet theirs.

It is because this new economic thought puts the citizen and the common good at the centre of its concerns that we believe that political decision-makers should give it their attention. The 'new economics' is based on a vision which could be a source of inspiration for politicians: the systematic development of individual responsibility, the effective preservation of resources and the environment, respect for qualitative and not just quantitative values, respect for feminine values and the need to place ethics at the heart of economic life.

It is for all these reasons that the Forward Studies Unit asked a well-known figure, James Robertson, to try to synthesize these movements favouring an 'alternative economics for sustainable development'. Is there a new economics, what are its starting points and its references, its priorities and its practical propositions?

When the study was presented on 5 May 1997, a lively debate ensued with the 30 European officials present.

I believe the type of debate that this book will provoke to be necessary and useful for future development of thinking in this important subject.

Jean-Claude Thébault
Director, Forward Studies Unit

List of abbreviations

EU	European Union
EMU	European Monetary Union
ESDI	European Sustainable Development Initiative
G7/G8	Group of Seven (Eight) Rich Industrialized Countries
GATT	General Agreement on Tariffs and Trade
GDP	Gross Domestic Product
GEF	Global Environment Fund
ICT	Information and Communication Technology
IMF	International Monetary Fund
IPTS	Institute for Prospective and Technological Studies
LETS	Local Exchange Trading Systems
LIF	Local Investment Fund
NAFTA	North American Free Trade Area
NGO	Non-Governmental Organization
ODA	Official Development Assistance
OECD	Organisation for Economic Cooperation and Development
R&D	Research and Development
SDR	Special Drawing Rights
TOES	The Other Economic Summit
UNCED	United Nations Conference on Environment and Development
UNDP	United Nations Development Program
WB	World Bank
WTO	World Trade Organisation
WWF	World Wildlife Fund

About the author

James Robertson studied history, philosophy and classics at Oxford. In the 1950s and 1960s he worked as a British government policy-maker in Whitehall – first on decolonization and development, accompanying Prime Minister Harold Macmillan on his 'Wind of Change' tour of Africa in 1960; then in the Cabinet Office. Then, after three years in management consultancy and systems analysis, he set up and led an inter-bank research organization for the British banks. Between 1965 and 1973 he took part in enquiries into British government, civil service and parliament, and London's future as a world financial centre.

Since 1973, he has worked independently as a writer and adviser on alternative futures and economic and social change. He has lectured in many countries on the post-modern transition to socially equitable and ecologically sustainable development. In 1984 he helped to set up The Other Economic Summit (TOES) and the New Economics Foundation (NEF). With his wife, Alison Pritchard, he edits the twice-yearly newsletter *Turning Point 2000*.

His books include:

- *The Sane Alternative: A Choice of Futures,* Robertson, 1978, 1983;
- *Future Work: Jobs, Self-Employment and Leisure after the Industrial Age*, Gower/Temple-Smith, 1985;
- *Future Wealth: A New Economics for the 21st Century*, Cassell, 1990;
- *Beyond The Dependency Culture*, Adamantine, 1997.

His publications for TOES and the New Economics Foundation include:

- *Health, Wealth and the New Economics* (1985);
- *The New Economics of Information* (1989);
- *Benefits and Taxes: A Radical Strategy* (1994).

Many recent published articles include:

- *The Fallacy of Single-Level Control: Local economies in a changing global environment*, Futures, March 1993;
- *Electronics, Environment, and Employment*, Futures, June 1995.

He retired in 1996 as a Trustee of the New Economics Foundation, and completed a Visiting Fellowship at the Green College (Oxford) Centre for Environmental Policy and Understanding.

Introduction

'There was a time when by the "new economics" was meant the Keynesian economics, which was notable as a response to the depression of the 1930s. The new economics that is struggling to grow today is something very different. It constitutes our response to a new set of problems which was only dimly perceived earlier, but has steadily grown in urgency over the last quarter of this century. It attempts to put forward new ideas about how to organise the foundations of a sustainable economy at this juncture in history when there are clear signs that the global economy cannot move much further along the accustomed paths of industrial growth without ending up in total disaster. For the true welfare economist the horizons of enquiry are shifting again in a new direction. . . . The study of wealth and welfare stands at a new crossroads.'

Amlan Datta (1997)[1]

This book was commissioned by the Institute for Prospective Technological Studies (IPTS) on behalf of the Forward Studies Unit of the European Commission in order to provide 'a value-added review of recent alternative-economic-paradigms work as it pertains to sustainability, with a particular emphasis on the practical/policy implications'.[2]

Sustainable development has been defined in many different ways. Perhaps the best known definition is that in *Our Common Future* (page 43) – 'development that meets the needs of the present without compromising the ability of future generations to meet their own needs'.[3] Conventional economic progress fails to meet the needs of many millions of people today and compromises the ability of future generations to meet theirs. The new economics reflects the growing worldwide demand for new

1

ways of economic life and thought that will conserve the Earth and its resources, and empower people to meet their own needs and the needs of others.

There is thus a close affinity between sustainable development and the new economics. Both recognize the need for change in today's direction of development and today's ways of economic life and thought. In general, the new economics brings a more radical perspective to sustainable development, and implies more far-reaching changes, than the mainstream perspective. For example, it emphasizes the need, as part of the shift to sustainable development, to move:

> *away from a state-centred or business-centred economic system, towards a more people-centred system, and away from money-measured growth as the principal economic target and measure of success, towards sustainability in terms of real-life social and environmental and economic variables.*

But the dividing line between the new economics and the mainstream is not static. The pattern of the past quarter-century has been that, as independent voices have spread awareness of the need to shift to sustainable development and what this will involve, mainstream opinion has shifted – after a time lag – to incorporate new economics approaches. As this process continues – the forward thinkers moving ahead of the mainstream and mainstream opinion moving to catch up – no firm boundary can be drawn between the evolving mainstream agenda for sustainable development and the policy implications of the new economics. There will always be some new economics policy proposals that have reached the mainstream agenda,[4] while others – still politically unrealistic to policy makers and policy analysts, and professionally off-limits to conventional economists – have still to reach it. Among examples discussed in this book, environmental taxation has come on to the mainstream agenda in the past few years, the Citizen's Income is nearly there, site-value land taxation may still have a little way to go, and – in spite of the attention being given to LETS (see Chapter 4) – multi-level currency systems and interest-free money may be rather further off.

PURPOSE OF THIS BOOK

The purpose of the book is to report what the new economics is about and what some of its key policy implications are. More specifically, the aims are as follows.

- to outline the *background and principles* of the new economics, and their connection with sustainable development;
- to indicate their *application to important fields of policy*;
- to suggest that a number of *key 'framework' policies* will promote sustainable development in all these fields;
- to identify such policies for *taxation and public expenditure*;
- to note the need for other framework changes – local, national and global – in the *monetary and financial system*;
- to discuss the implications of certain other changes, e.g. in ways of *measuring and accounting for economic activity*;
- to identify certain practical and theoretical *long-term questions* (such as the implications of a shift from income growth to cost reduction as a driving force in the economy), which call for study and analysis – but not at the expense of delaying urgently needed policy changes;
- also included is an illustrative *bibliography* and resource list.

This book should not be read primarily as a plea for the new economics, nor as an attempt to justify its principles and policy implications. Readers are not necessarily expected to agree with the statements in it, such as 'more self-reliant local development will play a key part in the transition to a sustainable future' (section 2.5). Throughout, the many statements made in that form should be taken as reports of the developing views of new economics

3

supporters and thinkers, and their implications (of which policy makers need to be aware), rather than as assertions to be accepted or rejected.[5]

A distinction has to be made between, on the one hand, those in the new economics movement who aim to subordinate the money-based calculations and values of conventional economics to real-life considerations and ethical and political values, and – on the other hand – the more mainstream economists who aim to extend conventional economic methods to environmental issues. In practice, no hard and fast line can be drawn between the two. But the purpose of the book is to deal primarily with the first.

SOME RELEVANT FACTS OF LIFE

Governments and government agencies (including the European Commission) are themselves an important part of the problem. Existing public policies – e.g. for agriculture and transport, but in most other fields also – give powerful encouragement to unsustainable development. Governments and government agencies will come under steadily increasing pressure to rectify that. Being advised to put one's own house in order may not be the advice one most wants to receive. But policy makers need not see it as negative and unexciting. For example, the proposed changes in existing structures of taxation and public expenditure aim not merely to remove incentives to unsustainable development, but to replace them with powerful positive incentives in favour of sustainable development.

Another fact to be reckoned with is that most government policy makers have traditionally been expected to keep within their own departmental boundaries – to specialize in their own subject and respect one another's 'turf'.[6] Inter-departmental co-ordination has generally had the limited aim of achieving acceptable trade-offs between conflicting departmental policies developed separately. The conventional policy-making approach to sustainable development follows this pattern, and tends therefore to be fragmented. The new economics identifies possibilities of a more systemic and synergistic kind – systemic because, for example, changes in framework policies for taxation and expenditure will encourage shifts towards sustainability in many departmental policy fields (such as farming and food, travel and transport, energy, patterns of work, more self-reliant local development, etc.), and synergistic because a shift towards sustainability in each of those fields will encourage a comparable shift in the others. Governments and government agencies will come under increasing pressure to show that they understand the need and scope for synergistic policies of this type, and have the integrative capability to develop them and introduce them and implement them.

Third, because it takes time for mainstream opinion to adjust to the new economics, some of its more important policy implications will not yet be acceptable to many of the people who need to consider them. Until compelled to take them seriously, why should policy makers do so in the midst of all the urgent calls on their time and energies? As I know from personal experience with the Central Policy Review Staff of the UK Cabinet in the early 1970s, it is one thing for a forward studies unit to commission studies on future possibilities, and quite another thing to motivate policy makers to pay attention to the findings. Nonetheless, policy makers will do well to be aware of the growing momentum behind the new economics approach, even if they do not yet accept it themselves. Pressure will continue to grow for changes in economic life that will give primacy to the needs of people and Earth, and for changes in economic thought that will provide new concepts of economic efficiency and progress. Policy makers will want to be ready to respond to the implications.

PRINCIPLES OF THE NEW ECONOMICS

As Chapter 1 outlines, the contemporary new economics movement has gathered increasing momentum since the UN conference on the environment in 1972, the publication in the same
year of *Only One Earth*, *The Limits to Growth* and *Blueprint For
Survival*, followed in 1973 by *Small Is Beautiful: Economics As If
People Mattered*. During that quarter-century, new economics
principles have crystallized. They contrast directly with the conventional economics approach.

They include the following:

- systematic *empowerment* of people (as opposed to making and
  keeping them dependent), as the basis for people-centred
  development;
- systematic *conservation* of resources and environment, as the
  basis for environmentally sustainable development;
- evolution from a 'wealth of nations' model of economic life
  to a one-world model, and from today's international economy to an ecologically sustainable, decentralizing, *multi-level
  one-world economic system*;
- restoration of *political* and *ethical* factors to a central place in
  economic life and thought;
- respect for *qualitative* values, not just quantitative values;
- respect for *feminine* values, not just masculine ones.

These principles are relevant to every *area* of economic life and
thought (such as farming and food, travel and transport, etc),
and to every *level* (ranging from personal and household to global)
and every *feature* (such as lifestyle choices and organizational goals).
Applying the principles to each area, level and feature of economic
life can yield a comprehensive checklist for a systematic policy
review.

The following features of the new economics underline its
direct relevance to policy making.

- It is *normative*, focusing on action to create a better future for people and Earth.
- It is based on a *realistic* view of human nature, recognizing that people are both altruistic and selfish, co-operative and competitive. Thus it recognizes that evolving the economic system to reward activities that are socially and environmentally benign (and not the reverse, as at present) will make socially and environmentally responsible choices the easier choices for people and organizations.
- It is about *transforming* today's economic life and thought, shaping a new mainstream for the future, not just about promoting secondary alternatives co-existing with today's mainstream.
- It is dynamic and developmental, working for changes in the direction of progress, not to a blueprint for a final destination.
- As already mentioned, its approach is *systemic and synergistic*. It looks for 'framework' policies that will promote sustainable development in every field and it recognizes that more sustainable development in one area will be closely linked with sustainable development in every other.
- It is *critical and constructive*, based on recognition that effective opposition to conventional economic development and thought is a necessary part of the transformation, but that constructive alternatives must also be proposed.
- It recognizes the need to combine *short-term* with *long-term* change. Short-term policy changes to meet current mainstream policy objectives should be such as will help to open the way to new policy objectives and more fundamental changes in the longer term.

THE STATE, THE MARKET AND THE CITIZEN

Mainstream economic and political opinion has assumed that there are three types of economy:

- a state-centred command economy;
- a business-centred free-market economy; and
- a mixed economy, based on a sharing of economic power and influence between government, business and trade unions – the 'social partners' – who are expected to co-operate more or less closely with one another.

The people-centred economic system on which sustainable development will have to be based differs from all those producer-orientated and employer/employee-centred systems. This means that the collapse of the state-centred communist model is not seen to have consolidated conventional Western business-dominated capitalism, but to have helped to open the way to its transformation.

The roles of the market and the state will continue to be important. The role of the market will be to serve the needs of citizens in environmentally sustainable ways. The role of government will be to develop a financial and regulatory framework designed to encourage personal and local self-reliance, economic efficiency and enterprise, social justice, and environmental sustainability. But a sustainable economy will also recognize the prime importance of those activities that are carried out neither for profit in the market nor by employees of the state. An active 'third sector' alongside the public and private sectors, and an active 'informal economy' based on unpaid interpersonal co-operative self-reliance, will constitute a province of citizen activity free from the impersonal constraints of the state and the market. The growing importance of voluntary organizations, citizens' groups and non-governmental organizations (NGOs) is evidence that this trend is already under way.

Conventional economic policies have focused on the interests of business and finance, employers and trade unions, and other organizations, as indispensable intermediaries on whose activities people must depend. New economic policies for sustainable development will focus more directly on people as active citizens. Recycling a significant proportion of public revenue directly to citizens as a Citizen's Income (see Chapter 3) will be an example.

AREAS OF POLICY

Chapter 2 is about the implications of sustainable development across a range of policy areas. These include farming and food, travel and transport, energy; work, livelihoods and social cohesion; local development; technology; business; health, and law and order.

A number of 'framework' policies are noted that apply to all these policy areas. They include the following:

- restructuring the *tax system* in favour of environmentally benign development and higher levels of employment and useful work;
- introduction of a *Citizen's Income* paid unconditionally to all citizens in place of many existing social welfare benefits;
- termination of *subsidies and other public expenditure programmes* which encourage unsustainable development;
- introduction of *public purchasing policies* which encourage contractors to adopt sustainable practices;
- development of more *self-reliant local economies*, involving (among other things) support for local banking and financial institutions, local means of exchange (local 'currencies'), local shops, and easier access for local people to local 'means of production';
- development of *indicators* to measure economic, social and environmental performance and progress;
- development of *accounting, auditing and reporting procedures* (and other *accreditation* procedures) to establish the sustainability performance of businesses and other organizations;
- *demand reduction* policies (e.g. for transport and energy), and the need to consider their implications;
- changes in the existing *international trading regime*, to encourage sustainable forms of trade.

CHANGES IN TAXES AND WELFARE BENEFITS

Perhaps the most important complex of policy proposals discussed in this book involves:

- ecotax reform, i.e. shifting the tax burden away from employment, incomes and activities that add value, and on to activities that subtract value by using energy and resources (including the capacity of the environment to absorb pollution and waste); and
- replacing existing tax allowances, tax reliefs, and many existing social welfare benefits with a basic income paid to all citizens as of right – a Citizen's Income.

The pressures to restructure the present systems of taxation and welfare benefits are strong and growing stronger. They encourage inefficient use of resources – over-use of natural resources and under-use and under-development of human resources. They discourage employment, and also useful unpaid work. Means-tested benefits discourage saving, as well as the earning of income. They create poverty and unemployment traps that lead to increasing social exclusion and rising costs for education, health, and law and order. Already expenditure on the welfare state is at crisis level in many industrialized countries.

For the future, an ageing society will find it even more difficult to tax fewer people of working age on the fruits of their employment and enterprise in order to support a growing number of 'economically inactive' people. In the medium term at least, a competitive global economy will continue to create pressure for lower taxes on personal incomes and business profits in order to attract inward investment.

Ecotax reform is now well and truly on the mainstream agenda, following the European Commission's White Paper on *Growth, Competitiveness, Employment* of December 1993. But, a difficulty about it is that, if existing taxes on the fruits of people's work and enterprise are simply replaced with environmental taxes, the effect will be regressive. Poor people will be hit relatively harder than richer people. Ecotax reform can only be viable on a significant scale if it is part of a larger package, other components of which will counteract that regressive effect. Land site-value taxation and a Citizen's Income can serve that purpose.

Chapter 3 outlines how this combination can be evolved. It will reflect an understanding that a sustainable society is one:

- which does not tax people for what they earn by their own useful work and enterprise, by the value they add, and by what they contribute to the common good;
- in which the amounts that people and organizations are required to pay to the public revenue reflect the value they subtract by their use of common resources; and
- in which all citizens are equally entitled to share in the annual revenue so raised, partly by way of services provided at public expense and partly by way of a Citizen's Income.

There will be the makings here of a new social compact for a new era. The social compact of the full-employment age is breaking down. The time is passing when the great majority of citizens, excluded from access to land and other means of production, and from their share of common resources and values, could nevertheless depend on employers to provide them with adequate incomes in exchange for work, and on the state for special benefit payments to see them through exceptional periods of unemployment. A new social compact is needed that will encourage all citizens to take greater responsibility for themselves and their contribution to society. In exchange, it should recognize their right to a share of the 'commons', so enabling them to become less dependent than they are today on big business and big finance, and on employers and officials of the state.

PUBLIC SPENDING

The second part of Chapter 3 discusses the implications of sustainable development for public spending.

It needs to be understood that the whole array of public expenditure programmes and taxes existing at any one time (together with the non-existence of public expenditure and taxation on other things) constitutes a framework which helps to shape market prices and thereby rewards certain kinds of activities and penalizes others. This framework should be designed to encourage economic efficiency and enterprise, social equity, and environmental sustainability. It should also be designed to minimize uncertainty and disruption caused by need for *ad hoc* interventions in the workings of the market.

The following specific conclusions are noted.

- Public purchasing policies should encourage sustainable and equitable practices on the part of contractors, thus contributing to sustainable and equitable practices throughout the economy.
- Systematic reviews should be carried out and published on the sustainability effects of all public subsidies (and other relevant public expenditure and tax differentials), with the aim of eliminating subsidies that favour unsustainable development. (One estimate has put the total value of environmentally damaging subsidies in Britain alone at £20bn a year – which suggests a huge figure for the EU as a whole.)
- Temporary subsidies for sustainable development initiatives such as green investment funds should be considered. But reducing the existing bias of taxation and public expenditure in favour of unsustainability is more important.
- Systematic reviews should be carried out and published on the possibilities for re-orientating public spending programmes, with the aim of preventing and reducing environmental and social problems before the event, rather than concentrating on trying to clean up and remedy their effects afterwards.

One further point should be noted. As new patterns of taxation and public spending help to shape a more people-centred (as well as a more environmentally sustainable) economy, they will enable people to meet more of their needs for themselves and one another. Over time, that will allow reductions in public spending and so, in turn, reductions in the revenue required from taxation. That will fit well, since taxes on the use of energy and resources will, if successful in terms of reducing their use, have the effect of thereby reducing their own tax base.

MONEY AND FINANCE

The money and finance system is conceptually more complex and more clouded in professional mystery than most other fields of policy. It has been difficult for policy makers in other fields, and for NGOs, to get to grips with it. Strategic understanding still has to crystallize about the changes implied in the sphere of money and finance by a shift to people-centred, sustainable development.

However, as Chapter 4 describes, it is clear that the way today's money and finance system works is damaging to people and the Earth. It contributes to unsustainable development in two main ways:

- it systematically transfers resources from poor to rich.
- the money-must-grow imperative drives production (and therefore consumption and investment) to higher levels than would otherwise be needed.

As the damaging nature of the money and finance system becomes more apparent, a post-modern perspective on money – appropriate to the Information Age – is beginning to come into focus. Increasingly people are starting to ask:

- What is the money and finance system for? What functions do we need it to perform?
- For whose benefit does it exist? Who does it belong to?
- Why does it work so inefficiently and unfairly at present?
- Can it be more intelligently designed and deliberately developed to provide people with a fair and efficient scoring system to facilitate transactions between them, by recording and exchanging the claims they are entitled to make on one another for goods and services now and in the future?

Specific issues include:

- proposals for multiple and multi-level currency systems;
- proposals to mitigate the unsustainable effects of interest and debt;
- prospects for deregulated currencies and quasi-currencies;
- the possible implications of electronic money;
- the need to apply sustainability accounting, auditing and accreditation procedures to financial institutions; and
- the role of green and social investment, and the role of local banking and microcredit institutions, in the shift to sustainability.

Each of these is discussed in Chapter 4. Developments in each will have an impact one way or another on sustainable development in many different spheres. Each is an area in which further understanding and action are needed. Policy makers, not only in the monetary and financial area, need to become more familiar with them.

THE GLOBAL ECONOMY

As outlined in Chapter 5, the peoples and governments of Europe have a full part to play in the further evolution of global economic governance over the coming years. We can help to shape global economic policies and institutions in support of people-centred, environmentally sustainable development all over the world. The contribution we can make is threefold. We can:

- show that we are committed to reorienting our own way of life towards sustainable development;
- ensure that our own national and European activities in the spheres of international trade, investment and aid contribute to sustainable, not unsustainable, development in other parts of the world; and
- participate effectively with the rest of the international community in the building of new global institutions, and the restructuring of existing ones, in support of sustainable and equitable development.

Sustainable development will involve reversing what has been a central feature of world economic development hitherto. That is the relatively higher growth rate of international trade than of world economic output, and – to an even greater extent – the relatively higher growth rate of international financial flows. In that sense the new economics shares Keynes' well known sympathy with '*those who would minimize, rather than with those who would maximize, economic entanglement between nations*'.

As countries around the world move, as in due course they will, toward a new framework of relative prices created by changes in taxation and public expenditure as already outlined, this will encourage more self-reliant economic activity at national and local levels. That will help to reduce international trade and international financial flows.

Further policy implications include the following:

- At the national and European level, European governments and the European Commission should regularly and systematically review their policies and spending programmes on export promotion, outward investment, aid, and technology

15

transfer, with the aim of ensuring that they contribute to sustainable, not unsustainable, development in recipient countries. They should also consider possible ways of making it easier for their own countries' consumers and investors to support 'fair trade'.

- In cooperation with their own NGOs and international NGOs, European governments and the Commission should actively help to shape the further evolution of global economic policies and institutions, which will help all participants in economic activity worldwide to move as rapidly as possible towards sustainability.

In particular, this means adopting policies to:

- evolve through the World Trade Organisation (WTO) a regulatory framework for international trade which will rule out unilateral protectionism while encouraging self-reliant, conserving development worldwide;[7]
- cancel the unrepayable debts of the poorest Third World countries;
- develop a system of global taxation, preferably based on charging nations for the use they make of common global resources, and using the revenue partly to provide all nations with a per capita 'citizen's income' (which would replace much of today's development aid to Third World countries), and partly to fund the UN system and its operations;[8]
- develop a more effective system of management for the international monetary and financial system, possibly including the introduction of a global currency; and restructure the institutions of global economic governance, to co-ordinate the policies and activities of the World Bank, International Monetary Fund (IMF) and WTO more closely with other parts of the United Nations system, under the supervision of a new world economic council more widely representative than the existing Group of Seven (G7).

FROM GROWTH TO SUSTAINABLE DEVELOPMENT

Chapter 6 discusses a number of further issues arising from the prospect of a shift to sustainable development:

- The shift to sustainability calls for new indicators for measuring economic achievement, new procedures for accounting for it, new methods of assessing policy options that will improve on cost/benefit analysis, and a review of the meaning of economic efficiency as it affects every field of policy.
- A key question arising from the development of environmental and resource taxation is whether the principle underlying it should be seen as the internalization of costs now externalized, or as payment for the use of common resources. This is not just a theoretical question. The answer to it will provide practical guidance for policies on the further introduction of environmental and resource taxes.
- A widespread shift of emphasis from raising incomes to reducing costs could be part of the shift to sustainability. This could have serious implications for the financial system. Practical contingency planning is needed. It might also be helpful to commission theoretical research on the difference between a conventional economic system (driven by rising incomes and the money-must-grow principle – see 4.1) and an economic system in transition to sustainability (in which saving costs becomes a driving force).
- The changing conceptual foundations of science and economics will influence one another in ways relevant to sustainable development. This is a topic that could usefully be explored further.

CONCLUSION

The new economics has to be taken seriously. Its orientation to people and the Earth focuses it on sustainable development. It proposes new policy approaches and new ways of meeting today's economic, social and environmental needs. It may seem to threaten powerful established interests, and to call in question existing institutional structures, existing organizational values, and existing expansionist tendencies in government, business and the careerist professions, and conventional economic orthodoxy. But that is what any effective approach to sustainable development will involve.

Many Europeans today are unclear about Europe's future world role, and are therefore unclear and unenthusiastic about Europe's future. But Europe could play a vital part in leading the world toward a people-centred, environmentally sustainable future, if the necessary vision and political will could be mobilized among our policy-making élites.

The new economics also points to the only effective way to deal with our own European problems of environmental damage, unemployment, rising poverty and crime, growing 'underclass', and declining social cohesion. Its policy implications demand attention.

Notes

1 Amlan Datta, *For a Quiet Revolution*, Papyrus (Calcutta), 1997.
2 See Annex A for the background to the assignment and the terms of reference. Throughout the report, I refer to 'alternative-economic-paradigms work' as 'the new economics'.
3 WCED (1987). For definitions of sustainable development see Annex A and IPTS (1995).
4 A number of the policy issues discussed in this book are, for example, already being studied under the auspices of European Commission Directorates-General.
5 It would have been tedious to have prefaced every statement of

that kind with some such phrase as 'most supporters of the new economics argue that' or 'some new economics thinkers conclude that'.

6 Much the same is true of academics and academic disciplines.

7 In spite of growing pressure against free trade, there are strong arguments against national protectionist policies to impose unilateral restrictions on international trade; and it would probably be impossible to restrict or prohibit international financial flows by unilateral national legislation and regulation.

8 If global taxes include the proposed 'Tobin' tax on currency exchange transactions, that could – depending on the level of the tax – help to reduce international financial flows.

Chapter 1

The new economics

'An economic system is not only an institutional device for satisfying existing wants and needs but a way of fashioning wants in the future.'

John Rawls (1971)[1]

1.1. BACKGROUND

The new economics reflects the growing worldwide demand for a new direction of economic development and progress that will be people-centred and Earth-centred. The new patterns of economic life and organization that this will necessarily involve will empower people to meet their own and one another's needs, and to conserve the Earth and its resources, now and for the future. This new way of economic life will be based on new assumptions, theories and values about economic activities and progress. With many other people, I see this as an aspect of a larger historical change, marking the end of the modern and the transition to a post-modern age, and as an aspect of a new global consciousness. But it does not have to be seen that way.

The following are among the key features of the challenge now faced by the global human community:[2]

- Modern society is going through a fundamental transformation, reflected in many signs of institutional and cultural

breakdown and in myriad constructive social innovations and experiments.

- At the heart of our major problems and current dilemmas lie relatively unquestioned assumptions, including an especially powerful set of assumptions that inform our economic institutions and values.
- Worsening national and global environmental crises, social problems and institutional breakdowns are probably best viewed not as separate 'problems' to be handled with specific technological, managerial, or legislative 'solutions', but as *symptoms* of an underlying disorder.
- The fundamental changes that must occur will inevitably involve the major concentrations of power in modern society, particularly the financial, business and government institutions.

One of the critical factors in this transition period will be how individuals and organizations in these sectors interpret and respond to the forces for change.

Much of the primary motive force and guidance for the necessary transformation will come from the growing 'third sector' of NGOs, voluntary associations, non-profit organizations, and other informal groups operating outside the private and public sectors.

The growing sense in people around the world that modern society is not working now and is not sustainable in the long term, stems in large part from the tendencies of the global socio-economic system toward:

- systematic destruction of the natural environment,
- systematic destruction of community,
- systematic transfer of wealth upward,
- systematic marginalization of persons, communities and cultures,
- systematic erosion and denial of the sense of the spiritual or sacred, and
- systematic creation of learned incapacity and helplessness.

22

Looking back from the perspective of 2050, what happened in the first half of the 21st century may look something like the following.[3]

'At the heart of the most pressing global dilemmas lay two assumptions:

1. *that the economy should be the dominant institution in society;*
2. *and that economic logic and economic values could guide decisions toward socially desirable outcomes.*

These assumptions were increasingly viewed as flawed, even by a growing number of people in the fields of business and economics. Noting that the fundamental concepts of business and labour, of employment and welfare theory, of liberal and Marxist analysis, were all based in production-focused society, they questioned a host of problematic implications:

- *that economic production was the de facto goal of society (increasingly questionable when a major challenge was precisely the modern economy's capacity to overproduce);*
- *that knowledge and an ever-increasing fraction of overall human activity should be treated as commodities in the mainstream economy;*
- *that the individual's primary relationship to society was through a job;*
- *that social thinking was to be dominated by concepts of scarcity, commercial secrecy, competition, consumption, and monetary exchange; and*
- *that natural and human resources were to be assessed solely in terms of their economic value.*

Such critiques would have carried little weight if social needs were being met and ecosystems protected, but by this time it was plainly apparent that tinkering with the system was not going to solve some basic systemic dilemmas. The increasing intensity of the challenge of environmental sustainability, challenges associated with

23

> *development in the poorer countries, and a growing rich-poor gap both within and between countries, contributed to the legitimacy challenge faced by the dominant institutions in the global economy.'*

1.2. RISE OF THE NEW ECONOMICS MOVEMENT

The following sketch of the rise of the contemporary new economics movement over the past quarter-century (mainly as it has evolved in the UK) will convey a sense of its growing momentum.[4]

As it has developed, the new economics has recognized an affinity with earlier thinkers like Robert Owen, John Ruskin, William Morris, Tolstoy and Gandhi, and with earlier alternatives to the mainstream, such as Fourierism and other decentralized socialist movements of the early 19th century, the Georgist movement that originated a century ago with the land tax ideas of Henry George, and the Social Credit and Distributist movements of the 1920s and 1930s.

But the contemporary new economics movement itself goes back only to the late 1960s and early 1970s. E.J. Mishan (1967) drew attention to the costs of economic growth and criticized 'growthmania'. *Blueprint For Survival* (1972) endorsed John Stuart Mill's view that 'a stationary state of capital and wealth' would be a very considerable improvement on our present condition. It would imply 'no stationary state of human improvement. There would be as much scope as ever for all kinds of mental culture, and moral and social progress'. *Only One Earth* (1972) and *The Limits To Growth* (1972) came out at the time of the United Nations Conference on the Human Environment in Stockholm. E.F. Schumacher's *Small Is Beautiful,* about 'economics as if people mattered', and Herman Daly's *Toward A Steady-State Economy* both appeared in 1973. Meanwhile, in *Deschooling Society* (1971) and subsequent books, Ivan Illich had been showing that modern progress creates scarcity and dependency by depriving people of the capacities and resources to judge their own needs and to meet them for themselves and one another.

By the mid-1970s increasing numbers of people had begun to perceive signs of a breakdown in the old order. Many experienced these *'symptoms of tomorrow'* as Higgin (1973) had described:

> *'Once you have experienced disbelief in the reality and values held by most of those about you and of the organisations you spend your life in, you cannot undo it, no matter how you try. If need be, you can go on existing in the old reality, but never again with vitality and commitment.'*

Some feared that the human factor in the global crisis, 'the combination of political inertia and individual blindness that constitutes the Seventh Enemy' (Higgins 1978), might make it impossible to prevent an impending global catastrophe of terrible dimensions arising from six other crises – population explosion, food crisis, resource scarcity, environmental degradation, nuclear abuse, and science and technology unleashed.

But there was also an optimistic side. As people discovered others who shared their sense of what was happening, they began to perceive, not only that the old order was showing signs of breakdown, but that a range of emerging new trends might eventually converge to create a breakthrough to a new one. These trends included – among others – environmentalism, concern for Third World development, decentralism, alternative technology, feminism and futures studies. As, by the later 1970s, conventional economic imperatives were increasingly seen as the cause of many of the world's problems, practical new initiatives – like the Intermediate Technology Development Group – were taking shape, and attention was turning to the positive aspects of 'the end of economics' (Henderson 1978) and new paradigms of wealth, growth and power (Robertson 1978).

The new economics has been out of sympathy with the rightward shift to the monetarist, 'free-market', business-centred economic policies of Thatcherism, Reaganism and their aftermath in the 1980s and early 1990s. A major landmark in its reaction to them was the first meeting of The Other Economic Summit (TOES) held in London in 1984 concurrently with the annual Economic Summit of the Group of Seven rich industrial countries (G7), to draw attention to the G7's inadequacy as a world economic council and to the irrelevance of the annual G7 summit agendas to the real economic concerns of people all over the world. TOES brought together people from many countries, South as well as North, representing citizen initiatives and groups concerned with development, social justice, poverty, feminism, alternative technology, environmental and other issues. It helped to stimulate international support for the new economics approach. Edited papers from it and the 1985 London TOES meeting were published (Ekins 1986). TOES became a regular annual counter-summit to the G7. The New Economics Foundation was set up. Participants in the first TOES have subsequently played prominent parts in many countries in support of sustainable people-centred development.

The 1990s have seen a rising tide of books about the need for a new economics, with such titles as *The Economic Revolution* (Hoogendijk 1991), *The Green Economy* (Jacobs 1991), *The Violence of the Green Revolution* (Shiva, 1991), *The Growth Illusion* (Douthwaite 1992), *Wealth Beyond Measure* (Ekins 1992), *The Development Dictionary* (Sachs 1992), *The End of Economics?* (Buarque 1993), *In the Wake of the Affluent Society* (Latouche 1993), *Feminist Perspectives on Sustainable Development* (Harcourt 1994), *The Death of Economics* (Ormerod 1994), *Earth Politics* (von Weizsacker 1994), *Whole Life Economics* (Brandt 1995), *Beyond Growth* (Daly 1996), *Building a Win-Win World* (Henderson 1996).[5]

The 1990s have also seen important advances in the capacity of the NGO community, national and international, to advise, lobby and campaign for change in many fields of economic policy. Internationally, NGO participation played a key role in the 1992 Earth Summit and subsequent UN Summits on social development, women's issues, population and habitat, and continuing NGO pressure on the World Bank has helped to bring about the beginnings of change in its policies towards poverty and the environment in Third World countries. In Europe, NGOs like Friends of the Earth (FOE) and the World Wide Fund for Nature (WWF) have been campaigning for new policies for a sustainable Europe. In Britain last year over thirty leading NGOs and voluntary organizations came together in the Real World Coalition, recognizing that their wide-ranging concerns all call for a political and economic programme based on the goals of sustainability, social justice, democratic renewal and community regeneration. Its published statement (Jacobs 1996) questions the conventional model of economic growth, reassesses the meaning of economic and social progress, and proposes policies for moving to a new path of development.

As the new economics has crystallized, and as new mainstream institutions like the UN Commission on Sustainable Development and the UK Government Panel on Sustainable Development have been set up, their shared concerns have brought them closer together. Both recognize that big changes are needed in conventional economic activity, policy, organization and theory.

The new economics perspective on sustainable development implies more far-reaching changes than the mainstream perspective. For instance, the mainstream still sees economic growth as prerequisite to sustainable development, whereas the new economics sees economic growth as a misleading policy goal – in principle neither desirable nor undesirable *per se*, but in practice often environmentally and socially damaging. (See 6.1 and Annex A.)

But this gap between new economics and the mainstream is not static. The lesson of the past quarter-century is that, as independent voices have spread awareness of what the switch to sustainable development will involve, mainstream opinion has shifted – after a time lag – to incorporate new economics insights and proposals. As this process continues – the forward thinkers and activists moving ahead of the mainstream, and mainstream opinion moving to catch up – there is no firm boundary to be drawn between the policy implications of the new economics and the evolving mainstream agenda for sustainable development. At any particular time there will be some new economics policy proposals that are reaching the mainstream agenda and others – still seen as politically unrealistic by policy makers and policy analysts and professionally off-limits by mainstream economists – that have not yet done so. The situation in 1997, for example, is that environmental taxation has come on to the mainstream agenda in the past few years, the Citizen's Income is nearly there, site-value land taxation and multi-level currency systems may still have a little way to go, and interest-free money is probably rather further off.

A key question is how to accelerate this process of *'turning the margins into the mainstream'*,[6] in order to minimize human suffering and environmental damage and smooth the transition from unsustainable to sustainable development.

1.3. PRINCIPLES

Many people are involved in the new economics movement. They are rapidly increasing in numbers. They come from all over the world. Their specific concerns and activities are diverse. Collaboration between them develops as a largely uncoordinated process.

Naturally there are differences of emphasis among them. Some are mentioned later in this section. The new economics is not a narrowly defined or precisely delimited body of doctrine or understanding. But the following summary would carry a fair measure of agreement.

The new economics is based on *principles* that contrast with the conventional economic approach, e.g.:

- systematic *empowerment* of people (as opposed to making and keeping them dependent), as the basis for people-centred development;
- systematic *conservation* of resources and environment, as the basis for environmentally sustainable development;
- evolution from a 'wealth of nations' model of economic life to a one-world model, and from today's inter-national economy to an ecologically sustainable, decentralizing, *multi-level one-world economic system*;
- restoration of *political* and *ethical* factors to a central place in economic life and thought;
- respect for *qualitative* values, not just quantitative values;
- respect for *feminine* values, not just masculine ones.

All the principles listed above are closely related to the shift to sustainable development. Each has policy implications. Taken together, and applied to every *area*, every *level* and every *feature* of economic life and thought, they can provide a comprehensive basis for sustainable policy making.

Areas of change include:

- farming and food;
- travel and transport;
- energy;
- work, livelihoods and social cohesion;
- local development, including cities and countryside and the built environment;
- technology;
- businesses and other enterprises and organizations;
- health;
- law and order;
- globalization, trade, investment and aid;
- money and finance: incomes, taxes, public expenditure, currencies, debt, banking, etc.

Levels at which change is needed include:

- personal and household;
- neighbourhood and local community;
- district and city;
- regional (sub-national);
- national;
- international/continental;
- global.

Features of economic life and thought in which change is needed include:

- lifestyle choices;
- organizational goals and policies;
- methods of measurement and valuation, e.g. accounting;
- research and theories.

As suggested, these principles, areas, levels and features offer a check-list for a *systematic* policy review. Applying the principles to each area of policy for which a department of government (or a Directorate-General in the European Commission) is responsible, would present no great conceptual problem. Initially, it could be done in a rough and ready, commonsense way, to identify possible changes in policy which deserve more thorough analysis. If, given the political and organizational will, this process were carried out in every department of a government (or every DG in the European Commission), the results would provide policy makers with advance warning of future policy changes for which pressure is likely to grow.

However, the application of new economics principles to all these different areas, levels and features of economic life and thought requires, not just a systematic approach, but also a *systemic* (or holistic) approach. A new policy that helps to promote changes needed in one area will often help to promote the changes needed in another. The effect of a restructured tax system on future developments in agriculture, energy, transport, patterns of work, and local economic development is an example. (See Chapters 2 and 3.)

The interconnections between the changes needed for a shift to sustainability in different areas also constitute an *ecology of change*, (and a corresponding ecology of inertia). Change achieved in one area (e.g. energy) will help to ease change in others (e.g. agriculture, transport), and change frustrated in one area can help to frustrate it in others. This creates great scope (and also great need) for *synergy* in the design and implementation of new policies. Unfortunately the conventional departmental structure of governments and government agencies makes it difficult for them to capture this synergy. The departmentalization of faculties and disciplines in universities and research institutes creates comparable difficulties for them too. This is one reason why so much of the innovative policy work on the new economics of sustainable development has hitherto come – and, to be realistic, will probably continue to come – from outsiders and NGOs, and not from within professional staffs in government and academe.

The following further features of the new economics should be noted.

- It *focuses on action* to create what it sees as a better future for people and Earth. It is normative. It questions whether economics could be an objective, value-free science. (Nature abhors a vacuum. The values vacuum created by the pretensions of conventional economics to be value-free has been occupied by the values of power and greed.)
- It takes a *realistic view of human nature*. It recognizes that people are both selfish and altruistic, competitive and co-operative, lazy and enterprising. It aims to evolve the economic system into one that rewards activities that are socially and environmentally benign and penalizes activities that are not. Thereby it aims to make responsible choices the easier choices for people

and organizations of all kinds. (It is also realistic enough not to – as Gandhi put it – 'dream of systems so perfect that no-one will need to be good'.)

- It is about *transforming* today's economic life and thought. It is concerned to create a new mainstream for the future, not secondary alternative ways of life and thought co-existing in parallel with today's mainstream. It sees the shift to sustainable development as an aspect of this transformation.

- Its perspective is *dynamic and developmental*, not static and once-for-all. It seeks changes in the direction of progress, not a final destination. It does not try to lay out a blueprint for a perma-nent state of affairs, let alone a Utopia, to be achieved in the 21st century. It sees the development of people and commun-ities as an integral part of the development of the economy, society and the wider world, including the natural world.

1.4. SOME DIFFERENCES OF EMPHASIS

Differences of emphasis within the new economics movement reflect issues of importance. They include the following:

- *Critical and Constructive.* Some supporters of the new economics concentrate on criticizing and campaigning against conven-tional economic policy and theory. Others concentrate on developing alternatives, and working with the mainstream to put them into practice. In fact, many NGOs are now more creatively involved in policy development than the official policy makers are. The oppositional stance and the constructive stance are both important. Though apparently conflicting, in practice they support one another. Powerful public criticism of the existing state of affairs and active opposition to schemes proposed by business and government can help to create conditions for policy change. A recent example is the impact on transport policy in the UK of opposition to new motorway building.

- *Short-Term and Long-Term.* Achieving comparatively straight-forward policy changes fairly quickly has to be done in close cooperation with business, government and other branches of the mainstream. Helping to create a new climate of under-standing, to which the mainstream will eventually have to respond with more radical policy changes, has to be done more independently. Again, there need be no conflict between people working in these two different ways, especially if the short-term changes help to open the way to the more fundamental ones. Take work and local development as examples.
  - *Work.* Creating more jobs is a policy goal already on the mainstream agenda. Changes in taxation (see sections 2.4 and 3.1) will help to achieve it. But the same changes, combined with a Citizen's Income, will also open the way to the more radical change of encouraging people who don't have jobs to commit themselves seriously to unpaid family and neighbourhood work – so helping to improve the upbringing of children, the self esteem of the people concerned, and local social cohesion.
  - *Local Development.* Internationally competitive businesses, in a globalized economy increasingly based on the use of information technology and other advanced technologies, cannot provide enough jobs to prevent local economic and social decline in many places. But the international competi-tiveness of an economy suffers if it has to carry the high costs of widespread local decline. In that immediate context, more self-reliant local socio-economic development is becoming an economic policy goal. Taking a longer-term view, it will eventually come to be seen as absurd to base the world's economic life on the assumption that people cannot do useful work or provide a decent living for them-selves and one another, except by competing with people on the far side of the planet to produce goods and services which nobody strictly needs. When that happens, flourishing self-reliant local economies, originally fostered to support

national competitiveness in the global economy, will be valued for their own sake.

- *Economists and Non-economists.* The new economics movement includes both economists and non-economists among its supporters. They tend to take different approaches. The economists recognize that, until recently, economic analysis has failed to take proper account of environmental and social benefits and costs. Their priority is to extend economic analysis to those hitherto neglected areas. Many of the non-economists (and a growing number of economists too) believe that, although economic calculations may play a useful subordinate role, they now play too large a part in policy decisions, and often provide a disingenuous justification for socially and environmentally damaging decisions that favour powerful interest groups. The priority for these people is to subordinate economic analysis to transparent processes of ethical and political decision-making.

- *Compulsion and Freedom.* Some people tend to see compulsion and government intervention as the natural means of achieving people-centred sustainable development. Others tend to look first to empowerment – enabling people to be more self-reliant, and less dependent on big government, big business and big finance to meet their needs and dictate their lifestyles as they now do, unsustainably. To some extent, the difference reflects a leaning towards either traditional socialist or traditional liberal ideas. It links with the question whether regulations or economic instruments are to be preferred. It also links with the question whether, so far as sustainable development is concerned, government (and governmental agencies like the European Commission) should be seen primarily as part of the solution or primarily as part of the problem.

This last question has important implications for public policy. Should the emphasis be on new government interventions and spending programmes that positively support sustainable development? Or should it be on scrapping existing government policies and programmes that support unsustainable development? In contrast to the interventionist tendency of conventional left-wing thinking, much new economics opinion tends to support greater freedom for individuals, localities and small enterprises and less dependence on government, as well as on big business and finance. But greater freedom must not include the freedom to diminish the freedom of others. It is a principal responsibility of government to ensure that it does not. One way or the other, government's role is vital.

That brings us to the question of the relative roles of the state, the market and the citizen.

1.5. THE STATE, THE MARKET AND THE CITIZEN

Conventional opinion in the 20th century has assumed that there are three types of economy:

- a state-centred command economy;
- a business-centred free-market economy; and
- a mixed economy, based on a sharing of economic power and influence between government, business and trade unions – the 'social partners' – who are expected to co-operate more or less closely with one another.

These producer-orientated, state-centred, business-centred and employer/employee-centred models of the economy all differ from the people-centred model on which sustainable development will be based.

The implications of this include the following:

- The collapse of communism should not be seen as 'the end of history', heralding a future permanently dominated by conventional free-market capitalism. Quite the opposite. Removal of the threat of Soviet state-dominated communism has removed the need, in the words of Hilaire Belloc's cautionary tale, 'to keep a-hold of Nurse for fear of finding something worse'. It has made it possible to look much more critically at the faults of global capitalism. In that light, the collapse of communism can be seen as the first of two major changes marking the end of the producer-orientated economic development of the late modern era, the second being the coming transformation of Western business-dominated capitalism.

- Although the roles of both the market and the state will continue to be vital, a sustainable economy will be one in which the importance of activities carried out neither for profit in the market nor by employees of the state is also seen as vital. An active 'third sector' alongside the public and private sectors, and an active 'informal economy' based on unpaid, interpersonal, co-operative self-reliance, will create a province of citizen activity free from the impersonal constraints of the state under conventional communism/socialism and from the impersonal constraints of the market under conventional capitalism.

- Policies for people-centred, environmentally sustainable development will focus more directly on the needs of people than conventional economic policies have done, and less directly on the interests of business and finance, employers and trade unions, and other organizations which conventional economic policies have assumed to be indispensable intermediaries on whose activities people must depend. The proposal to recycle a significant proportion of public revenue directly to citizens as a Citizen's Income (Chapter 3) is a specific example. More generally, policy makers will increasingly tend to treat people more as citizens, and less as consumers and employees (or potential employees). The conventional economic policy emphasis on consumers and consumption, employees and employment, will increasingly be seen as an aspect of an unsustainable production-orientated society. For the short term, it will be desirable to help to meet people's consumer demands and needs for jobs in more sustainable ways than at present. For the longer term, the aim will be to help people to stop regarding themselves primarily as consumers ('I shop, therefore I am') or as employees ('I have a job, therefore I am').

- Against that background, a key role for government in the transition to sustainable development over the coming decades will be to develop a monetary and financial framework (involving changes in taxation and public expenditure and other aspects of the monetary and financial system), designed to encourage personal and local self-reliance, economic efficiency and enterprise, social justice and environmental sustainability. A particular aim will be to enlarge the freedom and capacity of people to meet their own and one another's needs sustainably – with support from, rather than dependency on, the institutions of big business and finance.

This institutional framework will reflect the following perceptions:

- first, enclosure – the exclusion of most people from a share in the value of common resources developed by Nature and society at large, and the expropriation of their value by a more privileged minority – is a basic cause of today's poverty, inequality, and destructive treatment of the natural world; this needs to be put right;
- second, people and localities and nations need a degree of built-in protection and insulation from instabilities in the national and global economy that are outside their control;
- third, the framework should be based on maximum universality, maximum transparency and minimum complexity;[7] and
- fourth, in the course of time, as people become less dependent on business and financial corporations for jobs and goods and services, and as people find themselves in a stronger position to negotiate with business and finance on more equal terms, it should become possible to allow the market to operate more freely and flexibly in some respects than today.

The more specific policy implications of these points are discussed in later chapters.

Notes

1 John Rawls, *'A Theory of Justice'*, Oxford University Press, 1971, p259.
2 This and the following paragraph are paraphrased from a *Progress Report* and *Draft Scenario* (looking back from the year 2050), both of August 1996, from the *Pathfinding Collaborative Inquiry* being carried out by Willis Harman and Thomas J. Hurley of the Institute of Noetic Sciences (see Annex B). Willis Harman died earlier this year. I first met him in 1976, when his *An Incomplete Guide to the Future* was published. He took part in the first meeting of The Other Economic Summit (TOES) in London in 1984. He was a principal founder of the World Business Academy, as well as President of the Institute of Noetic Sciences.
3 Quoted from the same Progress Report – see note 2 above.
4 It is necessarily a short and subjective sketch. It reflects a British perspective, and a personal one. Other people would see it differently. One day a proper history will be needed. Meanwhile, it would be interesting to see comparable summaries from other European countries.
5 This is a short selection of books on general aspects of the new economics. Other important books on specific aspects are referenced in the following sections.
6 Tony Long in WWF (1995), p133.
7 Maximum universality means that, as far as possible, regulatory and financial provisions should apply to everyone, and not be targeted at particular groups or interests. Maximum transparency means that the way they operate and their effects should be clear. Minimum complexity means that a proliferation of specific provisions, and a need for special government interventions, should be minimized. How the system operates, as a whole and in its parts, should be as easy as possible to understand.

Chapter 2

A common pattern

'We do not use a different scheme, a different framework, on each occasion. It is the essence of the matter that we use the same framework on different occasions.'

P.F. Strawson (1959)[1]

The previous chapter outlined the principles of the new economics. This chapter briefly discusses a number of sectors of the economy to illustrate that the same set of 'framework' policies applies to all.

These framework policies include the following:

- Termination of *subsidies and other public expenditure programmes* which encourage unsustainable development.
- Introduction of *public purchasing policies* which encourage contractors to adopt sustainable practices.
- Restructuring the *tax system* in favour of environmentally benign development and higher levels of employment and useful work.
- Introduction of a *Citizen's Income* paid unconditionally to all citizens in place of many existing social welfare benefits.
- Development of more *self-reliant local economies*, involving (among other things) the encouragement of local banking and financial institutions, local means of exchange (local 'currencies'), local shops, and easier access for local people to local 'means of production'.

- Development of *indicators* to measure economic, social and environmental performance and progress.
- Development of *accounting, auditing and reporting procedures* (and other *accreditation* procedures) to establish the sustainability performance of businesses and other organizations.
- *Demand reduction* policies (e.g. for transport and energy), and the need to consider their implications.
- Changes in the existing *international trading regime*, to encourage sustainable forms of trade.

This section indicates the relevance of these framework policies. They are discussed in greater depth in later sections.

2.1. FARMING AND FOOD

Policy changes at international, national, regional (subnational), local and household levels are needed to eliminate world hunger, to improve food security, to enable people, localities and nations to become more self-reliant in the provision of food, and to improve the environmental sustainability of food production, distribution and preparation worldwide.

The aims include:

- more organic and less chemical agriculture and horticulture;
- more local growing of food for local consumption;
- a reduction in 'food miles', i.e. the distance travelled by food between producers and consumers, resulting in a reduction in the energy use and pollution associated with long-distance transport;
- encouragement for more people to grow more food for themselves and their families in gardens and allotments – i.e. for its use-value as opposed to its exchange-value – as an aspect of the informal as opposed to the formal economy;
- more opportunities for employment in agriculture and horticulture;

- the regeneration of more self-reliant local rural (and urban) economies, in which growing food for local consumption can play an important part (or, at least a greater part than at present);
- healthier food growing, food distribution and food preparation; and
- a fairer international trading regime, which will enable all countries, but especially developing countries, to achieve greater food security and a sustainable food sector as part of a sustainable national economy.

The policy implications include:[2]

- *removal of subsidies* that have effects damaging to health or the environment; raise land values artificially; encourage reductions in agricultural employment and favour capital- and energy-intensive farming; favour rich farmers against poorer ones and encourage the amalgamation of small farms into big ones; make it more difficult for new people to start up in farming unless they are rich; and support the dumping of excess food on to the world market, thus undermining food production and food security in developing countries;
- a *shift of taxation* away from employment and incomes to taxes and charges on land site-values, the use of energy and resources, and pollution;
- the introduction of a *Citizen's Income*, which will provide a degree of support for small farmers on low-value land, for people starting employment (including part-time employment) in agriculture and horticulture, and for people growing food unpaid in their gardens, allotments, etc;
- more *self-reliant development of local economies*, in which local growing of food for local consumption will play a significant part; and
- the introduction of a new *international trading regime* for food.

Other issues specific to farming and food include the following.

- *Biotechnology and patents on genetically engineered life-forms.* There is widespread opposition to the commercial development and monopolization of new animal and vegetable life-forms. Apart from the environmental risks, the economic and social effects are dependency-creating and socially divisive. For example, in countries like India the Green Revolution involved 'a shift from a farming system controlled by peasants to one controlled by agrichemical and seed corporations' (Shiva 1991, p64). Poorer peasants, who could not afford the new seeds and the machinery, fertilisers and pesticides required to grow them, had to become paid labourers of richer farmers who could afford them. The commercial monopolization of Earth's bio-diverse genetic inheritance is an unacceptable 'enclosure of the commons'. (The dependency-creating effects of techno-logical innovation as an aspect of conventional economic development are further discussed in 2.7 below. The concepts of enclosure of commons, and obligation to pay rent to the larger community for the use of common resources, have been mentioned in Chapter 1 and are discussed further in Chapter 3.)
- *Humane treatment of animals.* Animals are 'sentient beings', not just 'agricultural products' incapable of experiencing wellbeing and pain. We are ethically obliged to treat them humanely. Features of conventional industrialized agriculture which encourage inhumane treatment of animals – in their breeding, upbringing, treatment, transport and slaughter – are wrong and need to be corrected.
- *Vegetarianism.* Arguments in favour of vegetarianism must be taken seriously, from the viewpoints of human health and nutrition, animal welfare, the efficient conversion of natural resources into human food, and the damaging environmental and social impacts of certain types of animal husbandry – such as the conversion of tropical forests to large-scale ranching.

On the other hand, arguments in favour of organic mixed farming must also be taken seriously.

Other questions of more general application include the following.

- *Should subsidies be given* to initiatives in farming and food – and in other spheres – that contribute to sustainable development? There may be arguments for temporary subsidies as a transitional measure. But removing subsidies to unsustainable development is far more important. Removing the need for long-term subsidies of any kind will be an important goal of framework policies to create an economically, socially and environmentally sustainable economy. (For further discussion see Chapter 3.)
- *Purposeful consumers and investors.* A continuing general trend toward purposeful ('green', 'social', 'ethical') purchasing and investing will lead to increased demand for healthy food produced and distributed in humane and socially and environmentally sustainable ways, and will lead to increased investment in enterprises which supply it. This will be accompanied by a growing demand for reliable information, e.g. labelling of food products. The same applies to spheres other than farming and food. (For further discussion of ethical purchasing and investing, see Chapter 4.)
- *What does efficiency mean?* Efficiency is measured as a ratio between significant inputs and significant outputs. The greater the output in relation to the input, the greater the efficiency. The meaning of efficiency applicable in any particular case depends on what inputs and what outputs are regarded as most significant – what inputs is it most important to reduce, and what outputs is it most important to increase? Conventional economics has assumed that the most efficient farm is the one that produces the highest ratio between the profits earned (output) and the number of workers employed (input). Ratios between the calorific value of food outputs and the calorific

value of farm inputs, or between the amount of food produced (output) and the area of land farmed (input), have not been regarded as significant. Nor have the externalized costs of water, air and land pollution, soil erosion, impact on human health, destruction of wildlife and wildlife habitats, and rural unemployment. The meaning of economic efficiency in all sectors and aspects of economic activity now has to be reconsidered. (For further discussion see Chapter 6.)

2.2. TRAVEL AND TRANSPORT

Conventional development in travel and transport is environmentally damaging. It is also socially exploitative and divisive, in that it benefits richer people at the expense of poorer. Much new transport infrastructure, including new roads and airport runways financed through public expenditure, benefits the people who use them and profits the companies which build and operate them, but damages the environment and the quality of life of people who cannot afford to use a car or travel by air. A society physically, socially and economically structured around motor transport means significant loss of opportunity, liberty and quality of life for people without cars – especially children, women and elderly people – for whom cars make the streets unpleasant and dangerous. Tourism often damages the quality of life for poorer people in the places affected, especially in developing countries, while providing benefits for richer people (i.e. tourists) coming from elsewhere and yielding profits for businesses often based elsewhere. Hence the growth of 'tourism concern'.

Aims include:

- greater technical efficiency in transport systems, in terms of reductions in energy use and pollution, and improvements in safety standards and convenience;
- overall reductions in the currently externalized costs of transport and travel, including impacts on the environment, on

44

safety and health, and on quality of life – especially for people now excluded from many forms of travel and transport because of their cost;

- a shift from road and air travel and transport to rail, water, cycling and walking;
- a shift from individual car travel to collective (e.g. bus and train) travel (still sometimes referred to as a shift from 'private' to 'public' travel, even after the privatization of buses and trains); and
- reduced need for mobility (i.e. reduced demand for travel and transport), including less mobile patterns of working, living and trading (with less long-distance commuting and freight transport), and planning and design of the built environment to improve the accessibility (of shops, schools, hospitals, etc).

The policy implications include:

- the *removal of subsidies* (and other public expenditures) which support environmentally damaging and socially disabling forms of travel and transport;
- the *shift of taxation* away from employment and incomes to energy use and pollution, which will discourage environmentally damaging forms of transport;
- the introduction of other measures to *reduce the need for mobility*, including planning policies and regulations affecting the built environment,
- the introduction of a *Citizen's Income* which, by making it easier for people to work in and around their homes and local neighbourhoods, will reduce travel to and from work; and
- the development of more *self-reliant local economies*, that will reduce the need for long-distance transport and travel for business purposes.

The following general points, mentioned in the context of farming and food, also apply to travel and transport.

- Should subsidies be given to initiatives to improve the sustainability of transport and travel? (See 3.2.2.)
- Purposeful consumers and investors will provide support for a shift to sustainable transport. (See 4.4.2.)
- How is efficiency to be defined in the context of sustainable travel and transport? (See 6.3.)

Finally, the *need to reduce demand* for travel and transport has been mentioned. The need to reduce demand applies in many other fields too, including demand for energy, jobs, and services that deal with the consequences of ill-health, accidents and crime – as discussed later in this section.

That calls in question the future of economic growth. Although lower levels of production and consumption of marketed products and resources in many sectors – the further 'dematerialization' of economic activity – will be accompanied by some growth of marketed services to help people use products and resources more efficiently, there can be no certainty that the growth in the value of services will be high enough to offset the fall in the value of marketed products. The projected revival of informal, unpaid activity makes it the less likely. If a reversal of conventionally measured economic growth proves to be a necessary element in the shift to sustainability, it will not only upset conventional economic assumptions and calculations. It could also have serious implications for financial stability. This needs to be acknowledged and confronted ahead of time, proactively. (For further discussion see Chapter 6.)

2.3. ENERGY

Sustainable energy policies will be essential to the transition to sustainable development. Energy, like land, is a basic resource on which all economic activity depends. Energy-intensive activities are the cause of most types of pollution. Fair distribution of usable energy resources (or the values to be derived from using them) between people living in all parts of the world today and between present and future generations, implies a reduction in fossil fuel use by the industrialized countries of up to 90 per cent by the middle of the 21st century.

The need is twofold:

- to reduce *demand* for energy and
- to replace environmentally and socially damaging forms of energy *supply* with benign ones.

Specific aims include:

- greater technical efficiency in all forms of energy use, i.e. technological improvements enabling us to use less energy and less polluting forms of energy, while continuing to enjoy existing or better levels of other products and services (including energy services – heating, refrigeration, cooking, lighting, power, etc);
- new, less energy-intensive societal patterns of production and consumption, and living and working, which will further reduce the demand for energy – such as reduced travel to work, reduced 'food miles', and reduced long-distance transport of goods in general;
- shifting from energy supply based largely on non-renewable fossil fuels to renewable, solar energy;
- shifting from centralized energy supply systems – based on large power stations and electricity grids which are inefficient in terms of energy inputs and outputs, and over which people can exercise little control – to decentralized sources, such as passive solar heating, solar panels for heating water and generating electricity (by photovoltaics) for individual buildings (including people's houses), and local combined heat and power installations (CHP); and
- phasing out nuclear power, as a prime example of a centralized technology which is potentially disastrous for human health

47

and the environment, imposes incalculable costs and risks on future generations, distracts attention from energy conservation and the scope for decentralized energy supply, and whose use in most developing countries would involve continuing economic dependence on the industrialized world.

The policy implications include:

- *removal of subsidies* (and other public expenditures) that encourage increased energy use and the development and use of environmentally and socially unsustainable forms of energy;[3] and
- a *shift of taxation* on to energy use and off incomes and employment.

The following general points, mentioned in the context of farming and food, and travel and transport, also apply to energy.

- Should subsidies be given to initiatives to improve the efficiency of energy use and to encourage the development of sustainable forms of energy supply? (See Chapter 3.)
- Purposeful consumers and investors will provide support for a shift to sustainable energy. (See Chapter 4.)
- How is the efficiency of sustainable energy to be defined? (See Chapter 6.)

Energy, like transport and travel, provides a good illustration of the need to reduce *demand* as well as to encourage sustainable methods of *supply*. Conventional economics finds it difficult to grapple with this aspect of sustainable development. It continues to rely on growing demand for products and services, and people's growing dependence on them. Empowering people to consume less would be seen as sabotaging conventional economic progress. This perception is to be expected in a production-orientated economic world.[4]

Resistance to sustainable development has already been most clearly apparent in relation to energy. The energy industries and energy-intensive industries have forcefully resisted European proposals for a carbon-energy tax. But comparable resistance to the changes demanded by sustainable development in every other sphere may be expected from many organizations and individuals. How people, professions, businesses, industries, and governments are to be persuaded to embrace these changes as the way to a sustainable future is a strategic question of the first importance.

2.4. WORK, LIVELIHOODS AND SOCIAL COHESION

Tackling unemployment, poverty and social exclusion will be an essential part of a successful transition to sustainable development.

The situation may be summed up as follows.

- Conventional jobs will continue to be important. Policies that now discourage the employment of people, and encourage energy-intensive methods of production and distribution, should be changed.
- But it is unrealistic to assume that conventional jobs will provide useful work and livelihoods for everyone, and questionable whether that is still a desirable goal. Policies that will empower people to do useful work for themselves and one another are also needed.
- Much essential activity and useful work is unpaid. It includes parenting, household management, and active citizen participation in the life of the neighbourhood and local community and in national and international affairs. Policies should encourage and enable people to undertake work of that kind, other useful voluntary and informal work, and productive and rewarding leisure activities.

49

In other words, twin-track policies are needed

- to increase the supply of jobs and
- to reduce the need and the demand for them, by enabling people to enjoy a livelihood and engage in useful activity without having an employer to give them a job.

Specific policy implications include the following:

- *removal of subsidies* (e.g. for energy-intensive production processes) which have the effect of reducing employment and discouraging other forms of useful work;
- a *shift of taxation* away from employment and incomes to charges on the use of energy and resources and land-site values;[5]
- introduction of a *Citizen's Income*, to provide both a launching pad from which people can steadily build up paid work, and support for people doing useful unpaid work;
- measures to promote more *self-reliant local development*, encouraging the use of local work and local resources to meet local needs (see 2.5 for more detail);
- *education* to prepare people, not just for employment, but to manage their lives as adults and citizens, including managing their work and activities as individuals and as members of co-operative, community, neighbourhood and household groups; and
- facilitating *access to 'means of production'*, including land, work premises, equipment, capabilities and skills, and capital and credit.

It should be noted that different views about the future of work mean a difference of emphasis about priorities.

One view is that most people will continue to define work as what employees do for employers; and they will want a job. Sustainable development policies must therefore include measures to create full employment. Environmentalists often claim that environmentally benign policies will create many more jobs than they will destroy.

A second view accepts the need for policies that do not discourage employment, but sees it as unrealistic to rely on full employment coming back in industrialized economies, or being achieved in many developing countries. Continuing to rely on that could mean that many poor and socially excluded people would never be able to enjoy a decent livelihood or see themselves as full citizens. The precautionary principle requires policy makers to recognize this and introduce policies that will enable people to do useful work, gain a livelihood and take a full part in society, without having to find an employer to give them a job. Continuing to insist that most people should depend on employers to give them jobs is undesirable for another reason. It perpetuates the 'dependency culture' typical of an employer-centred, production-orientated, consumerist society. Policy makers should take the opportunity offered by the present worldwide crisis of unemployment to empower increasing numbers of people to organize and control their own sustainable work and livelihoods for themselves.

The third view foresees that, in many people's lives, work will be largely replaced by non-work activities, including parenting, household management and active citizen participation in local and national issues. In practical terms, the difference between this and the second view is largely one of definition. Instead of redefining work to include activities now regarded by conventional economic and political opinion as outside 'the world of work', as the second view does, the third continues to define work as excluding them. It therefore foresees a less important part for 'work' in people's lives, a more important part for 'activity', and thus a transition from 'work' to 'activity'.

2.5. LOCAL DEVELOPMENT

More self-reliant local development will play a key part in the transition to a sustainable future. Increased use of local work and local resources (especially in places where these are now under-employed, under-used and under-developed) to meet local needs (especially in places where these are now unmet) will have positive economic, social and environmental effects. More cyclical, less linear, patterns of local economic activity will reduce flows of imports into and exports out of many local areas; increase the local recycling, reconditioning and re-use of local waste materials and equipment; and, as regards financial flows, increase the recycling of local incomes and savings within the local economy.

For many years, national governments, the European Commission and the OECD have wrestled with the problems of economic crisis localities and regions, urban and rural.[6] That these problems are no nearer solution now supports the new economics view that they are *systemic problems*. Withdrawal from localities of local means of wealth creation and local capacity to meet local needs has been an inherent feature of the existing dependency-creating and centralizing system of economic institutions and policies. It has paralleled and reinforced the withdrawal from individual people and households of control over the 'means of production' and the capacity to meet their own needs by their own work. Change of a systemic character is needed to bring about a revival of local economies, as it is to deal effectively with unemployment and social exclusion for individuals and families.

Policy implications involve local, as well as national, government authorities. They include:

- *removal of subsidies and regulations* that favour non-local production and non-local provision of services;
- *shifting the burden of taxation* away from employment and incomes and on to land site-values and the use of energy; this will reduce land prices and internalize the costs of centralized

energy-intensive production and long distance transport, thus making access to land (and housing) more affordable to local people and encouraging local production for local consumption;

- the introduction of a *Citizen's Income*, which will make it easier for local people to take up part-time paid work, and to undertake unpaid work which contributes directly to environmentally and socially desirable activities in the local community economy;
- working out ways of encouraging *money to circulate locally* within a local economy, instead of leaking out of it;
- permitting local government authorities to issue *local currencies* and encouraging local community groups to set up LETS,[7] when too little national currency is in local circulation to provide the means of exchange required to support purely local economic transactions;
- encouraging the setting up of *local banking and financial institutions*, to enable local people to invest their savings in their own local economy;
- making sure that planning policies encourage local shops in villages, suburbs and small town centres, and discourage the monopolization of local retailing and other trading by branches of businesses based elsewhere; and
- developing *local indicators*, which will make it possible to monitor changes in the social, environmental and economic sustainability of the locality, including the impacts of branches of outside organizations on local employment, local production for local consumption, local flows of income and spending, saving and investing, and the local environment.

2.5.1. Local Agenda 21

Since the UNCED Earth Summit in 1992, the Local Agenda 21 process to promote sustainable development at the local level has been gathering pace. Sustainable development reports are now being published for increasing numbers of cities and rural areas. Two examples are the following.

Creating A Sustainable London (1996) points out that London has a giant 'ecological footprint' – the area needed to provide the resources it consumes and to absorb the wastes and pollution it creates. Much of that area, which is 125 times larger than London's own area and as big as the whole of Britain, is in fact in other countries. It could be significantly reduced if more of London's food was grown within its boundary or nearby, if more of the paper it uses was made from recycled materials, if its energy efficiency was increased and its fossil fuel consumption and pollution reduced, if a greater proportion of its wastes and sewage was recycled and composted, and if walking and cycling and travel by public transport replaced a significant proportion of existing car usage. (For further discussion on the concept of 'ecological footprint' see Chapter 6.)

Sustainable Gloucestershire (1996) looks forward to:

- sustainable farming, based on: small, mixed, family farms; more individuals growing some food for themselves; consumer support for organic farming; increased production of building materials and renewable energy from local farms; and conserving use of soil and water;
- a sustainable built environment, based on: raising the environmental performance of buildings; cutting travel, encouraging use of new communication technologies, and providing affordable public transport; conserving good land for food production; reducing demand for water; experimenting with the development of sustainable village communities; reviving more sustainable suburbs; and raising the quality of the urban environment;
- sustainable energy, based on: efficient and conserving use of energy; environmentally benign sources of energy supply; and greater local community responsibility for energy use and energy production projects;

- sustainable transport, based on: walking, cycling, buses, railways, reduced car use (especially for business travel and journeys to work), and shifting freight from road to rail (and water);
- minimizing waste and pollution, improving air and water quality, reducing noise levels, and cleaning up contaminated sites;
- a healthier future, based on: greater equity in opportunity, quality of life and employment; a strong sense of local community working together to meet local needs; a more even balance between work, essential activities and leisure; and work based nearer to home or at home; and
- new ways of conceiving economic life, and transforming economics into a system that will better serve humanity.

2.5.2. A difference of approach

Two different approaches to more self-reliant local development should be noted. One is that local communities should de-link unilaterally from the national and global economy, and develop self-reliant local economies as an aspect of their own revived autonomous local cultures.[8] The other, majority view is that, even if that were desirable, it would not be possible. Unless mainstream national and international institutions, policies, theories, values and attitudes change, efforts to establish significant numbers of autonomous local community economies are bound to fail. They could not survive the pressures of multi-national governmental institutions like the World Bank, the IMF and the European Commission, of national governments and central banks, and of large business and finance corporations – not to mention the mainstream media, education system, academics, scientists and professions – all subscribing to conventional assumptions about the nature of economic progress, and regarding it as their duty and interest to promote 'progress' of that kind.

This second view sees more self-reliant local development as a key element, but only one element, in the emergence of a new multilevel approach to economic organization (and political, governmental, social and cultural structure) worldwide. In accordance with the subsidiarity principle, it supports more self-reliant development at various subnational levels – regional, city and district, neighbourhood, and indeed household – as well as at national level. It recognizes not only the localization of economic decision making but also its globalization as aspects of a shift away from the conventional 'wealth of nations' focus on national economic policy making, and on inter-national economic competition as the engine of progress. It expects the post-modern economy to reflect an emerging consciousness that people are citizens of the world and of the locality where they live, as well as of the nation to which they belong. It thus supports the evolution of a new way of organizing and understanding economic life as a multi-level one-world system systematically geared to decentralized sustainable development.

These two views reflect a difference of emphasis rather than a disagreement about the policy implications. The main practical difference between them is that people holding the first will tend to concentrate on the practical grassroots aspects of initiatives within their locality, whereas people holding the second will also work for changes in mainstream institutions, policies and theories which now obstruct the success of initiatives of that kind.

2.6. TECHNOLOGY

The new economics is not opposed to technology. It is not Luddite – quite the reverse. It attaches great importance to the development and use of technologies that will:

- support future trends in farming and food, travel and transport, energy, work, and self-reliant development as already outlined;
- in other ways, also, conserve resources and reduce pollution, and

- enable people, local communities and developing countries to become more self-reliant and less dependent; and
- compete successfully in markets for empowering and conserving technologies, in a world economy committed to people-centred, environmentally sustainable development.

Those are not the kinds of technologies that have typically been developed in the past, and continue to be developed today. A feature of conventional economic progress has been and still is the development of centralizing, dependency-creating, unecological technologies. Centralized electricity power stations have been mentioned already. The high level of publicly funded R&D for nuclear power (against R&D for energy conservation and energy efficiency and solar energy technologies) illustrates the use of public funds to develop an unsustainable technology (see 2.3 above). The effects of this approach to technological development are also clearly seen in the sphere of biotechnology (see 2.1). It is significant that the development of military technologies plays so large a part in government programmes for science and R&D. One major criticism of the arms trade concerns the sale of military equipment to governments which use it against their own people.

The underlying reasons for technologies having developed on these lines are that:

- commercially profitable technological innovations are those that meet the wants of organizations and people with money to buy them;
- in a business-centred economy, governments support the development of technologies of that kind in order to help their national businesses to compete successfully in world markets;
- in state-centred economies, technologies were developed in accord with the requirements of centralized state bureaucracies;

- in the conventional production-orientated economy, whether business-centred or state-centred, it rarely if ever occurred to governments (and scientists, technologists and engineers) to develop technologies specifically designed to meet people's needs (people-centred technologies); and
- in an economy in which it has been possible to externalize environmental costs, the market has provided little incentive to develop environmentally sustainable technologies.

In short, the new economics recognizes that technology innovation is a double-edged sword. Communication and computer technologies, for example, can be developed to give people decentralized power to communicate with one another by phone and fax and e-mail and small decentralized newsletters and journals. (The use of faxes played a significant part in the popular movements that led to the break-up of the Soviet Union.) But communication and computer technologies can also be used for surveillance and manipulation, allowing Big Brother organizations of business and government to keep track of where people are and what they are doing, and allowing transnational corporate press and broadcasting media to shape international opinion on the important issues of the day.

Most of the main policy implications correspond to those already mentioned in other contexts:

- *stop subsidizing* (or otherwise supporting with public funds) the development and diffusion of technologies that encourage unsustainable activities or reinforce dependency and deprive people and local communities of the capacity to meet their own needs;
- insofar as they then continue to exist, *reorientate publicly funded R&D programmes* to support the development of conserving and empowering technologies;
- *shift the tax burden* off work and enterprise and on to the use of resources; and, by thus encouraging the use of people-

centred, resource-conserving technologies, expand the market for those kinds of technologies; and

- encourage the publication of *social and environmental reports and accounts* which, by stimulating organizations of all kinds to improve their social and environmental performance, will stimulate them to use socially and environmentally benign technologies, which will in turn stimulate producers to develop technologies of those types.

2.7. BUSINESS

In the 1980s and 1990s business and the business ethos have extended their power and range. This has accompanied an ideological shift in favour of 'free markets' and 'free trade' which, in practice, has meant freedom for large corporations to skew the world economy and national economies in their own favour, and diminish the freedoms of other actors in the global, national and local economies.

For example, intra-firm trade between the national components of transnational corporations (which constitutes about half of all international trade) is not subject to free trade. Free trade does not operate in important sectors of world trade such as food and agriculture, in which rich-country national interests predominate or which are largely controlled by transnationals. Nations have become dependent on the big business sector for sponsorship for sport, arts, culture and (to some extent) community projects. Local government relies on big businesses to provide finance for new local amenities, in return for favourable planning treatment, e.g. permission to build new superstores that put local shops out of business. (This is known as 'planning gain'.) National and local governments compete against one another to attract inward investment by transnationals, by offering them bigger subsidies and tax breaks at the expense of their own people. Backed by the governments of the most powerful nations, and having themselves become more powerful than many national governments, transnational corporations now 'rule the world'.[9]

There are two views within the new economics movement about the role of business in the shift to sustainable development.[10]

- One is that large business corporations must and can provide the main driving force for change; they will have to change profoundly if they are to do so; but there is reason to hope they will.
- The other is that that is an unrealistic hope; business corporations are trapped in a predatory world economy in which making the changes necessary for sustainable development would jeopardize their short-term survival and success, *unless their competitors are compelled to make the same changes too.*

For purposes of practical policy in the short and medium term, neither of these two views can be ignored. Business corporations are now so powerful for good or ill that they must be given every encouragement to support sustainable development – to become part of the solution instead of part of the problem. But the most effective forms of encouragement – probably the only really effective forms – will be those that change the rules of the game for the more backward-looking firms as well as the more forward-looking ones, and maintain fair competition between them. *Economic instruments* (see Chapter 3) must provide incentives for all companies to change in order to compete successfully in the market, and *regulations* must compel all companies to observe mandatory social and environmental standards.

2.7.1. Accounting, audit and accreditation

Such standards include the provision of information about the social and environmental impacts of businesses.

Interest in social and environmental accounting has grown in the last few years. These are now established as specialist fields in their own right. There is still some tendency to treat social and environmental reporting separately. And they are often criticized as largely cosmetic – as a shallow marketing ploy. But the need is becoming more widely recognized for businesses (and other organizations) to publish independently audited reports on their social and environmental performance. In practice, this does not yet extend to sustainability accounting or a sustainability audit. But, progressively over the coming years, systematic annual procedures should be developed to show, not just how a business is discharging its financial responsibilities to shareholders, nor even just how it is discharging specific social and environmental responsibilities to its other direct 'stakeholders' – including its employees, customers, suppliers and the local communities in which it operates – but also what positive and negative contributions it is making to local, national and global sustainability. This is of particular significance for banks and other financial institutions. Their ecological and social 'footprints' may not be immediately obvious, but are very important. (See 4.4.)

For businesses themselves, these accounting and auditing procedures will increasingly be part of the social and environmental management systems they need in order to retain the confidence of their various stakeholders and stay competitive. Increasing numbers of customers and investors will decide to buy from and invest in socially and environmentally responsible businesses, and this will help to change business priorities. But this could be a slow process, in the absence of government policies to accelerate it.[11]

Evidence of a company's social and environmental responsibility could also be provided by a system of accreditation. For example, a business that had the unanimous support of a recognized labour union, a recognized consumer organization, a qualified environmental agency and a leading development agency, could apply to be called a European Public Company. Those organizations would be required to testify that the company in question makes a positive contribution to sustainable development in

regard to its workers, its customers, the environment, and developing countries.[12]

2.7.2. Corporate structure

A logical extension of the need for social, environmental and
sustainability accounting and auditing would be the development
of more pluralistic and democratic corporate structures of ownership and control, in which the rights (and obligations) of all the
stakeholders (including future generations) would be represented
in the decision-making processes of big corporations and other
large organizations.[13]

It must be recognized that the corporate economy of the 21st
century will have to evolve more effective ways to organize and
motivate people to work in the larger interest than conventional
capitalism and socialism have done. But it is arguable whether
legislation to change company law for this purpose should have
priority in the context of sustainable development. The development of corporate accounting, audit and accreditation procedures
(see above) may be a better way forward for the time being.

2.7.3. A business-centred or people-centred society?

Mainstream research, consultancy and policy analysis about the
'greening of business' and the role of business in sustainable
development does not yet question business's present position of
economic primacy and power. It accepts the assumption that
business creates 'wealth' (but what is wealth?) and employment
(but can it create enough?); that people will continue to depend
on wealth and employment 'trickling down' from business; and
that business should therefore be first in line for subsidies, tax
breaks and other government favours designed to stimulate
desired economic activity.

The new economics looks to a more people-centred future,
and notes the growing evidence that citizens tend to be more

aware of the unsustainability of the conventional business ethos than business people are. On this interpretation, it is not 'greedy consumers' who are the crucial obstacle to sustainability. The crucial obstacles are on the production side – producers whose business survival and success depend on persuading consumers to buy more than they need, and the conventional economic assumption that a high level of production is the only way to provide people with work and livelihoods. Enabling people to work and gain a livelihood in other ways (see 2.4 above) will help to weaken that assumption. The proposed changes in the tax system (Chapter 3) can also help to persuade businesses to produce less and consumers to consume less.

2.7.4. Policy implications

The policy implications include the following.

- Governments which have not already legislated for *mandatory annual publication of social and environmental audits* by businesses of a certain size and type, should consider doing so.
- *Public purchasing policies* should require public contracts to be let only to businesses which publish satisfactory social and environmental audits, or are accredited under an approved scheme analogous to the labelling of environmentally approved products.
- Existing *subsidies to business* should be thoroughly reviewed. All subsidies that encourage unsustainable business activities should be stopped. Governments should also consider whether, as a general rule, economic efficiency, social cohesion and environmental sustainability might be better served by withdrawing all subsidies to business and distributing the expenditure instead to individual citizens as a contribution to a Citizen's Income.
- A *shift of taxation* away from employment and incomes and business profits to taxes and charges on land-site values, the

use of energy and resources, and pollution, will change prices throughout the economy and encourage more sustainable development in every kind of business.

2.8. HEALTH, AND LAW AND ORDER

Reducing demand will, as we have noted, be part of the shift from unsustainable to sustainable development. Reducing the demand for transport (by improving accessibility, reducing the need for mobility, and reducing food mileage), reducing the demand for energy (by energy-conserving technologies and less energy-intensive patterns of societal activity), and reducing the demand for jobs (by making it easier for people to gain a livelihood and do useful work, if they don't have a job), will be as important as supplying more sustainable modes of transport, more sustainable forms of energy, and more jobs.

This principle particularly applies in the fields of health and law and order. For that reason we look at those two fields very briefly here.

Conventional health policies and health services are, in fact, largely sickness policies and sickness services. They deal mainly with the effects of sickness and ill-health after they have occurred. Similarly, law-and-order policies and services (prisons, police, law courts, etc.) mainly deal with the after-effects of crime and disorderly behaviour. In other words, both are largely remedial. Successful healthy public policies, which helped to create a healthier society, would reduce the demand for conventional 'health' services. Successful law-and-order policies, which helped to create a more law-abiding society, would reduce the demand for police and prisons and law courts.

Sickness services and police and prisons will never be unnecessary – though it could be a useful exercise to spell out the form that such an imaginary Utopia might take. But a healthier and more cohesive, more law-abiding society cannot be created by policies, government departments and professions primarily concerned with 'health' (meaning sickness) and 'law and order' (meaning police and prisons and law courts). A healthier and more law-abiding society would clearly be a more sustainable society. But policies will be required from departments other than those conventionally responsible for health and law and order to reduce the causes of ill-health, crime and lack of social cohesion. They will include the departments responsible for farming and food, transport, energy, employment and work, etc., and the departments responsible for the financial and regulatory framework that helps to shape activities in those spheres.

Policy implications include the following.

- As a general rule, policies that *reduce demand* for particular types of goods and services, and create conditions that make them less necessary, will be an important feature of a sustainable society.
- Policies to *create a healthier, more socially cohesive, more law-abiding society* are examples. They call for review of existing policies, as outlined in this section, across a wide range of departmental responsibilities – for food and agriculture, transport, energy, employment and work, etc.
- Existing *subsidies and other public expenditures* that help to create ill-health, to weaken social cohesion, or to encourage anti-social activities, should be stopped.
- The *shift of taxation* already suggested will help to create a healthier, more cohesive society.
- So will the introduction of a *Citizen's Income*.

Again, the need to reduce demand highlights the possibility that reducing conventionally measured economic growth will be a feature of the shift to sustainable development. That presents a problem for conventional economic analysis and policy (see Chapter 6 for further discussion). It will also be resisted by the majority of people whose livelihoods, employment and professional careers now depend on supplying the categories of goods and services affected.

2.9. A BRIEF CONCLUSION

This section has aimed to show that the same set of framework policies will encourage the shift to sustainable development in many areas of the economy. These policies will be considered in greater depth in the next two chapters.

However, policy makers in fields like farming and food, transport, energy, employment and work, local development and spatial planning, technological innovation, business and industry, health, and law and order, must not regard the development of these framework policies for taxation and public expenditure, and other aspects of the monetary and financial system, as the specialist preserve of policy makers in the sphere of public finance. Influencing the form they take and the impact they make on real-life activities in every field will be an important responsibility for policy makers in those fields, as the transition to sustainability gathers pace.

Notes

1 P.F. Strawson, *Individuals: An Essay in Descriptive Metaphysics*, Methuen, 1959.

2 Specific implications for the European Common Agricultural Policy (CAP) were summarized in a four-page Briefing Note of November 1996 jointly produced by SAFE (Sustainable Agriculture, Food and Environment Alliance) and CIIR (Catholic Institute for International Relations). Proposed rewording of Article 39 of the Treaty of European Union to formulate new objectives for the CAP were published by WWF Europe in January 1996.

3 One example is the high level of UK government financial support over many years for nuclear energy R&D (research and development) contrasted with solar energy R&D.

4 From a feminist point of view, the priority given to new supply technologies over demand-reduction stems the interest in 'big toys' of the 'big boys' whose influence still predominates over that of women in the economic sphere.

5 Failure to tax site values raises land prices, thus making land unaffordable for people like potential small farmers and tradespeople who might otherwise work productively on it. It also encourages landowners to hold valuable land out of economic use in the hope of being able to realize speculative capital gains as land values rise.

6 My personal experience in this sphere has included a study of finance for local employment initiatives for DG V and OECD in 1985, and in 1996 I took part in a conference held by the Territorial Action for Social Cohesion (TASC) programme supported by DG V.

7 For further discussion of Local Exchange Trading Systems (LETS) see Chapter 4.

8 See Douthwaite (1996).

9 Korten (1995).

10 The first two chapters, respectively by Paul Hawken and James Robertson, in Welford and Starkey (1996), summarize these two views.

11 See Rob Gray, *Corporate Reporting for Sustainable Development*, in Welford and Starkey (1996).

12 Hulbert (1996), p12.

13 See, for example, Goyder (1987), Turnbull (1975 and later papers), and Robertson (1990), Chapter 8.

Chapter 3

Taxation and public spending

'The earth shall become a common treasury to all, as it was first made and given to the sons of men.'

Gerrard Winstanley (1649)

Chapter 2 identified changes in taxation and public spending as new 'framework' policies needed to encourage the shift to sustainable development across a wide range of economic sectors. This chapter discusses them in greater depth.

3.1. A RESTRUCTURED TAX SYSTEM AND A CITIZEN'S INCOME

The policy implications noted in Chapter 2 included:

- ecotax reform (i.e. a shift of taxation away from employment, incomes and savings, and on to resource-depleting and environmentally damaging activities),
- the further replacement of existing taxes by another resource tax – a tax on land site-values, and
- the introduction of a Citizen's Income.

Until recently, proposals in these three areas have been developed separately. They are now coming to be recognized as interconnected parts of a larger package. This would be phased in over a period of ten or fifteen years. The resulting change would reflect, and operationalize, a new social compact for a new era of sustainable development, in which full employment of the conventional kind, a welfare state of the conventional kind, and economic growth of the conventional kind, are no longer adequate policy goals and can no longer be maintained.

3.1.1. Ecotax reform[1]

An early rationale for environmental taxation was the 'polluter pays' principle. According to this, the 'externalized' costs of environmental damage inflicted on other people or on society as a whole should be 'internalized', i.e. paid by the person or organization inflicting them. Ecotaxes were seen as a way of making the polluter pay. As their practical and conceptual aspects are examined, the concept of ecotaxation is now broadening in two main ways.

First, it is broadening into the idea that people and organizations should pay for using natural resources. The capacity of the environment to absorb pollution and wastes is only one such resource. Energy taxes, water charges and traffic congestion charges are among those receiving attention. A tax on land is another obvious resource tax. Then, in addition to natural resources, there are institutional resources like the monetary system. Should users pay 'rent' to society for using them?[2] In principle, should people and organizations pay society for the benefits they enjoy from 'commons' of all kinds, i.e. resources and values that have been created by nature or society as a whole and not by the work or enterprise of the people who own them or use them? Should people pay for the value they subtract from the common pool?

Second, the original concept of ecotaxation has broadened into ecotax reform. This is concerned not only with the new taxes to be introduced, but with what existing taxes they should replace or reduce, and in what other ways the revenue from ecotaxes could best be used. The idea that revenue from ecotaxes could be used to reduce taxes on employment and incomes was given widespread currency in the European Commission's White Paper on *Growth, Competitiveness, Employment* of December 1993. It has been followed up in many studies since then.[3]

As the new economics proposal to use taxes as an instrument of environmental policy[4] has broadened into ecotax reform and is being explored by increasing numbers of mainstream economists, policy analysts and institutes,[5] the new economics is turning its attention to the next question: can ecotax reform be part of a more thoroughgoing restructuring of taxation and public expenditure to meet the needs of a sustainable, people-centred economy, in which site-value land taxation and a Citizen's Income would also play key parts?

3.1.2. Site-value land taxation

The proposal is to tax the annual rental site value of land. This is the rental value that a particular piece of land would have if there were no buildings or improvements on it. It is the value of the site, not including the value of developments carried out by the owner and his predecessors (which should not be taxed), but as provided by nature and as affected for better or worse by the activities and regulations of the community at large. Estimates for Britain in 1990 give a sense of the relative size of these values (£bn) for various land uses: housing 66.4; commerce 19.0; public services 10.2; industry 9.3; farm, woodland and forest 2.4.[6]

This tax has attracted the favourable interest of economists since Adam Smith. Ricardo (1817) pointed out that a 'tax on rent would affect rent only; it would fall wholly on landlords and could not be shifted to any class of consumers'. Its best known advocate was the American economist, Henry George. In 1879, in *Progress And Poverty*, he showed that to shift the burden of taxation from production and exchange to the value or rent of land would stimulate employment and the production of wealth;

71

the selling price of land would fall; land speculation would receive its death-blow; and land monopolization would no longer pay. Leading economists in recent years have agreed that the tax on economic rent is the most neutral and most efficient of all fiscal instruments, inducing no distortions and generating no loss of welfare:

- *'the least bad tax' (Milton Friedman);*
- *'cannot be shifted forward on to prices' (Samuelson and Nordhaus);*
- *'perfectly neutral with respect to the allocation of resources' (Lipsey).*[7]

In 1990, Nobel Prize-winning economists Franco Modigliani, James Tobin and Robert Solow were among a distinguished list of mainly American scholars who endorsed the principle that the rental value of land should be enjoyed by the community. They signed an open letter to Mr. Gorbachev, then President of the USSR, urging him not to sell publicly owned land but to raise government revenue by charging rent for it.[8]

Various political parties in Europe during the 20th century have included site-value taxation in their policies, and it provides a component of local taxation in a number of countries today. But mainstream policy analysts and economists show a strange lack of interest in its potential significance as a source of national revenue. Merely a case of professional group-think? Or, as some suggest,[9] the result of an intellectual conspiracy inspired by land-owning interests early this century? Or a bit of both?

Another factor may have been that, in spite of the merits of the site-value tax, some of its supporters in the past have done it no favours by insisting in an apparently unrealistic and utopian (and boring!) fashion that the site-value tax is the 'single tax' needed to finance all public spending, and that it should therefore replace *all* other taxes. Today, its more forward-looking advocates are presenting its merits more persuasively, as one resource tax among others. Their arguments for a system of public finance based on socializing (i.e. taxing) the rent of land *and other natural resources*, and privatizing (i.e. not taxing) people's wages and savings, seem wholly convincing. *Policy makers should seriously examine the potential of the site-value tax, as a resource tax that will contribute to economically efficient, socially equitable, and environmentally sustainable development.*

3.1.3. Citizen's Income (or Basic Income)

The proposal is to distribute a Citizen's Income (CI) – often known as a *Basic Income* – as a tax-free income paid by the state to every man, woman and child as a right of citizenship. It will be age-related, with more for adults than children and more for elderly people than working-age adults. CI for children will replace today's child benefit, and CI for the elderly will replace today's state pensions.

There will be supplements for disability, housing benefits, and other exceptional circumstances. Otherwise CI will replace all existing benefits and tax allowances. The amount of a person's CI will be unaffected by their income or wealth, their work status, gender or marital status.

The idea of a basic income goes back to Tom Paine in the 1790s and to the Fourierists and John Stuart Mill in the first half of the 19th century. In Britain, 20th-century interest goes back to the 1920s, when Major C.H. Douglas proposed Social Credit as a response to unemployment. More recently, support has come from distinguished economists. In 1990 Samuel Brittan of the *Financial Times* (one of the most respected financial and economic commentators in the U.K.) and Steven Webb (of the Institute for Fiscal Studies) argued that 'basic incomes need to advance beyond their present state of intense preoccupation to a minority and enter into the main current of political and economic discussion'.[10] In 1993 the late Professor James Meade, 1977 Nobel Prize-winner for Economics, who had argued for a Social or National Dividend back in the 1930s, advised the British Labour Party's Commission on Social Justice that a Citizen's Income should be introduced to supplement the restrained levels of pay needed to secure full employment. Support has also come from Conservative and Liberal politicians. In the last few years the Citizen's Income Trust has continued to generate active interest. Its quarterly Bulletin is an important source of information.

Equally influential support for a Basic Income has been growing in other European countries. A Basic Income European Network (BIEN) was set up in 1988. Its Newsletter, an indispensable resource, documents the growth of interest in Basic Income in Europe and around the world. Most recently, a study published in Ireland in April 1997 shows that a full Basic Income could now be introduced there over a period of three budgets, resulting in:

- nobody receiving less than the poverty line of income,
- all unemployment and poverty traps being eliminated,
- it always being worthwhile for an unemployed person to take up a job, and
- employers' annual payroll taxes being reduced by over £200 million.[39]

3.1.4. Taxes and benefits: The wider context

Pressures for a general restructuring of taxation and welfare benefits are growing stronger. Not only do the present systems fail to discourage environmentally unsustainable activities, and fail to encourage innovation for sustainability and a rising share of the growing world market for environmental technologies and services. More generally, they encourage people and businesses to subtract value, and penalize them for adding it.[12] They encourage inefficient use of resources – over-use of natural resources (including the environment's capacity to absorb pollution and waste), and under-use and under-development of human resources. They discourage both employment and useful unpaid work like parenting. Means-tested benefits discourage saving, as well as the earning of income. They create poverty and unemployment traps which lead to increasing social exclusion and rising costs for education, health, and law and order. Already expenditure on the 'welfare state' is reaching crisis levels in many industrialized countries.

For the future, an ageing society will find it even more difficult to tax fewer people of working age on the fruits of their employment and enterprise in order to support a growing number of 'economically inactive' people. In the medium term at least, a competitive global economy will continue to create pressure for lower taxes on personal incomes and business profits in order to attract inward investment.

In short, the need to reduce existing taxes on employment, incomes, enterprise, value added and savings, and the need to rationalize the social benefits system, are now coming on to the mainstream agenda of most industrialized countries, along with the need for ecotaxation. Like it or not, they are parts of the same package.

3.1.5. Avoiding regressive effects

A problem for ecotax reform is that, if existing taxes on the fruits of people's work and enterprise are simply replaced with environmental taxes, the effect will be regressive. Poor people, who do not pay the existing taxes, will be hit relatively harder than richer people who do. Ecotaxes by themselves, regardless of the taxes they replace, will have this effect if applied 'downstream' at the point of consumption. For example,

- value-added tax (VAT) on household energy hits poorer households, which do not have the money either for the extra tax costs or for the investment in energy efficiency necessary to reduce them; and
- similarly, fees and charges to reduce urban congestion will hurt small tradespeople who need to use their vehicles for their

work, but will be painlessly absorbed by users of chauffeur-driven limousines.

If ecotaxes are to replace existing taxes to any significant extent, these regressive effects will have to be minimized. This can be done in various ways, all of which are important.

- Ecotaxes should, as far as possible, be applied upstream. A prime example will be a carbon-energy tax (or a tax on fossil fuels and nuclear energy) *collected at source*. It will have three outstanding advantages. First, by raising the cost of energy-intensive activities it will also raise the cost of polluting activities, most of which derive from intensive energy use. Second, it will be clear that, by raising the cost of energy-intensive activities and products throughout the economy for producers as well as for consumers, it reduces incomes and wealth (salaries, dividends, capital appreciation, etc) derived from energy-intensive production, as well as raising prices of energy-intensive goods and services to consumers. In other words, it will clearly be universal in its application. Third, it will be administratively simpler than a widely proliferating variety of ecotaxes levied on distinct groups of consumers at many different points of consumption.
- Ecotaxes should be understood as including the proposed tax on the rental site value of land. Apart from its economic advantage as the least distortionary tax of all, this is a resource tax that is progressive. It will obviously hit rich people who own valuable land harder than poor people who do not.
- The revenue from ecotaxes should be used progressively. For example, a German study[13] concluded that if part of the revenue from an energy tax were recycled to households as an eco-bonus, the change would not only have positive economic and employment effects, but would reduce the net tax burden on low-income households; and a Swiss study[14] concluded that if the revenue from levying two Swiss francs per litre of

petrol were distributed to all adults as an ecobonus, people driving less than 7,000 kilometres a year would benefit, while people driving more would lose. (Note that if ecotax revenues grow substantially, and if a substantial proportion of them are recycled as ecobonuses to all citizens, the ecobonuses will begin to add up to a Citizen's Income.)

3.1.6. Targeting or universality?

In principle there are two alternative directions in which the social welfare benefits system might develop – towards stricter targeting or towards greater universality. That is well understood.

At first sight, it seems more sensible and less costly to target benefits strictly to those who really need them, rather than to distribute them to everyone. This is the direction in which much mainstream thinking has been moving. But targeting involves means testing. There is no other way to establish need and eligibility. And means testing has serious disadvantages. For example,

- means testing is perceived as demeaning and socially divisive;
- to avoid means testing, many people fail to take up benefits to which they are entitled;
- means testing tightens the unemployment and poverty traps, by reducing incentives to earn and save; and
- people who have earned and saved enough to disqualify themselves from means-tested benefits, feel resentment against those who have not – creating more social divisiveness.

Universality in the form of a Citizen's Income avoids these disadvantages, and is therefore preferable for both social and economic reasons. The problem is that, because it pays benefits to people who do not strictly need them, the total direct cost is higher than the cost of selective benefits based on means-tested need. However, the proposal to combine a restructured tax system with a Citizen's Income can solve that problem. It can deliver the advantages of both targeting and universality, and avoid the disadvantages of both.

The Citizen's Income will be distributed universally to all citizens as of right. Its effect will be progressive, because the same amount of money is worth relatively more to poor people than rich. But that amount of money (and more) will be clawed back from most of the people who are rich enough not to need it, via resource taxes whose effect will also be progressive – taxes on the ownership of land, and on the use of energy, the capacity of the environment to absorb pollution and waste, and other common resources. The result will be progressive because richer people own more land and enjoy more benefit from the use of common resources – that being the most important reason why they are richer.

The question of universality versus targeting applies to taxes as well as benefits. At this early stage in the development of environmental taxation there is a tendency to propose new ecotaxes targeted piecemeal at particular environmental impacts and the particular groups responsible for them. This risks being resented as discriminatory by the groups affected, as pensioners and low-income households in the UK resented the imposition of VAT on household energy. It also risks creating, as time passes, a confusing jungle of overlapping environmental taxes and charges.

Universality is a desirable principle for taxes as well as benefits. It would be achieved if all citizens were taxed on the values they enjoy from the use of common resources. Taxes on land site-values and on fossil and nuclear energy at source are two priority examples.

3.1.7. Towards a new social compact[15]

Policies for a sustainable future, then, should include ecotax reform, site-value land taxation, and Citizen's Income, as connected parts of a larger package based on:

- the introduction of a range of taxes and charges on the use of common resources and values, including – but not limited to – energy and the site value of land;
- the reduction, and perhaps the eventual abolition, of taxes and charges on employment, incomes, profits, value added, and capital; and
- the introduction of a Citizen's Income, to which ecobonuses would contribute, paid to all citizens as of right in place of all tax relief and many existing welfare benefits.

As already noted, the ecotax reform movement has been gathering strength in mainstream policy-making and academic research but still faces serious obstacles, while the movements for site-value taxation and Citizen's Income are growing stronger but yet have to mobilize mainstream momentum.

Over the next few years the potential synergies between the three will become more apparent. Beyond the practical arguments for treating them as a package, an integrating vision will emerge.

It will be a vision of a people-centred society – less employer-centred and state-centred than today's. Its citizens, more equal with one another in esteem, capability and material conditions of life than now, will all be entitled to share in the value of the common resources created by nature and society as a whole.

It will be a vision of a society:

- which does not tax people for what they earn by their useful work and enterprise, by the value they add, and by what they contribute to the common good;
- in which the amounts that people and organizations are required to pay to the public revenue reflect the value they subtract by their use or monopolization of common resources; and
- in which all citizens are equally entitled to share in the annual revenue so raised, partly by way of services provided at public expense and partly by way of a Citizen's Income.

79

While citizens of such a society will find it easier to get paid work, they will no longer be as dependent as they are now on employers to provide them with incomes and organize work for them. The modern-age class division between employers and employees will fade – as the old master/slave and lord/serf relationships of ancient and medieval societies have faded. It will be normal for people to work for themselves and one another. It will become an aim in many fields of policy to enable people to manage their own working lives.

The social compact of the employment age is now breaking down. The time is passing when the great majority of citizens, excluded from access to land and other means of production and from their share of common resources and values, could nevertheless depend on employers to provide them with adequate incomes in exchange for work, and on the state for special benefit payments to see them through exceptional periods of unemployment. A new, post-modern social compact will encourage all citizens to take greater responsibility for themselves and their contribution to society. In exchange, it will recognize their right to their share of the value of the 'commons', and so enable them to become less dependent than they are today on big business and big finance, on employers, and on officials of the state.

3.2. PUBLIC EXPENDITURE PROGRAMMES

The restructuring of welfare spending has been discussed above. We turn now to other public spending.

3.2.1. Public purchasing

The scale of public expenditure means that governments and other public bodies can influence the practices of organizations throughout the economy from which they purchase goods and services. They should use that influence through purchasing policies that encourage sustainable and equitable development.

One suggestion[16] is that accreditation under recognized environmental management standards might be made a requirement for businesses competing for public contracts. Other suggestions for the accreditation of businesses in the context of sustainable development were noted in 2.7.

3.2.2. A framework for the market

The need to remove subsidies that encourage unsustainable activities was noted under many of the headings in Chapter 2. One estimate[17] puts the total value of environmentally damaging subsidies in Britain at more than £20bn a year. If that is anywhere near the mark, it suggests a huge figure for the European Union as a whole.

Such subsidies are a perverse use of public money – i.e. citizens' money. How should governments (and the European Commission) respond? To mobilize public support for reducing these subsidies they should consider providing their respective Parliaments with a systematic yearly analysis, which would be published, of the possible effects on sustainable and equitable development of every subsidy provided under every spending programme. The analysis need not be economically sophisticated. Its aim would be to point out, for political and public discussion, examples of subsidies which common sense would suggest may be environmentally or socially damaging. By including representatives of relevant NGOs and pressure groups on the teams carrying out these analyses, their effectiveness would be enhanced.

But how are subsidies to be defined? What do they include? In addition to subsidies in the narrow sense, other forms of *de facto* subsidization artificially improve the competitive position of some products and activities against others by influencing market prices in their favour. Specific examples include:

- discriminatory taxes and tax exemptions, such as a higher rate of Value Added Tax on energy-saving equipment than on energy consumption (as in the UK);
- higher public spending on R & D in one field than in other related fields, as in the previously mentioned example of nuclear power in comparison with energy efficiency and energy conservation; and
- higher public spending on one type of transport infrastructure than on others, such as road compared with rail.

A wider example of subsidization (discussed in the previous subsection) is the *de facto* subsidy given by today's tax and benefits systems to energy-intensive production and distribution, and against employment and useful unpaid work.

In fact, the real issue is an even wider one. The whole array of public expenditure programmes and taxes existing at any one time (together with the non-existence of public expenditure and taxation on other things, and together with the existing body of legislation and regulation) constitutes a framework which helps to shape market prices, thereby rewarding certain kinds of activities and penalizing others.[18] This framework should be designed to encourage economic efficiency and enterprise, social equity, and environmental sustainability. It should also be designed to minimize uncertainty and disruption caused by a need for *ad hoc* government interventions in the workings of the market. The need to base it as far as possible on principles of universal applicability should be firmly in mind, as governments evolve a financial and legal framework for a market economy designed to meet the needs of sustainable development.

3.2.3. Subsidies for sustainable development?

Should specific subsidies and tax exemptions be given to activities and products that contribute to sustainable development?

In the short term there may be a case for this. For example, the favourable tax treatment recently introduced in the Netherlands for environmental investment funds (see 4.4.2 below) may encourage some people to consider investing their savings in environmentally benign products and services sooner than they would otherwise have done, and help to stimulate banks and other financial concerns to provide environmental investment facilities. As a temporary measure, it and other comparable subsidies and tax exemptions may serve a useful purpose.

But, if introduced at all, such subsidies and tax exemptions should be seen as strictly short-term. In each case the same question needs to be asked: What are the underlying reasons that make this subsidy necessary or desirable? In almost every case the answer will be that existing price distortions and subsidies – such as subsidizing users of energy and other resources by failing to price energy and resources highly enough – bias the economy against activities that contribute to sustainable development. It is better, for the sake of economic efficiency and environmental sustainability, to remove existing subsidies to unsustainable development than to introduce additional subsidies to counteract them. In the example mentioned, environmental investment will get a bigger long-term boost from ecotax reform than it will from a subsidy.

In a longer-term perspective, another point about subsidies and other forms of government financial support to businesses may become significant. Such subsidies discriminate in favour of commercial activities carried out by businesses against comparable activities carried out unpaid by citizens. Similarly, publicly financed services – including caring services – are subsidized against comparable services provided unpaid by citizens. In a business-centred, employer-centred, government-centred economy, taxing citizens in order to subsidize the activities of businesses, employers and government against comparable activities carried out by citizens for themselves and one another, has gone unquestioned. But, in a more people-centred economy, which aims to enable citizens to take more responsibility for themselves and one another, this discrimination in favour of the formal economy against the informal economy could come to seem increasingly questionable. This could reinforce other arguments for diverting to a Citizen's Income at least some of the money now spent on public expenditure programmes.

3.2.4. Prevention instead of cure?

A high proportion of government and other public expenditure is remedial. Its purpose is to deal with the effects of crime, social exclusion, ill-health, environmental damage, humanitarian disasters, breakdowns of law and order and outbreaks of civil war (as in former Yugoslavia and Rwanda), and so on – after they have occurred.

Although such after-effects as these will always arise and will always have to be dealt with, more attention should be given to preventing them happening and reducing their scale. The need to reorientate public policy and public spending towards the creation of conditions in which there will be less crime, social exclusion, ill-health, environmental damage, etc., was mentioned in section 2.8.

To take one specific example, there is growing evidence that diets, deficient in certain vitamins and trace elements and containing certain additives and other chemical substances, are a significant cause of attention deficit and hyperactivity in children, which can develop into anti-social and criminal behaviour as they grow older. The problem is that not many professionals in the police, prisons and other law-and-order services, in the education and employment services, in the medical and health (i.e. sickness) services, or in the drug companies, are interested in or knowledgeable about policies to promote healthier nutrition.

The first need is to establish:

- what the cost might be of a scheme to improve children's nutrition and identify particular foods which particular children should avoid, in order to reduce attention deficit and hyperactivity;
- what costs that scheme might save, which now arise from the various effects of hyperactive behaviour and the need to deal with them; and
- what benefits the scheme might bring to the children and their families and wider society in terms of improved quality of life, improved education, improved economic capabilities and generally improved life prospects.

That is just one example of many possibilities for a more proactive approach to policy for a healthier, more sustainable society. The more proactive approach needs to be generalized. A systematic annual analysis of public spending programmes could identify possibilities for re-orientating them toward reducing the need for the remedial activities for which they are now largely needed.

It must, however, be recognized that the professions which have grown up in the remedial fields of public service activity, and the bureaucracies and commercial interests which support them, are likely to be less than enthusiastic. For example, how many health practitioners and health officials are interested in and able to contribute to policies in spheres such as transport, energy, employment, planning, taxation, welfare benefits, and food and farming, which will help to create a healthier society? To generalize, the drive for a reorientation of public policy from cure to prevention cannot be expected to come mainly from today's remedial professions. It must come mainly from outside them.

3.2.5. Lower total public spending?

As the suggested changes in taxation and public spending are phased in over the years, people and localities will become better able to meet for themselves needs which are now met for them through public spending programmes. This will be an important feature of the shift to people-centred sustainable development. It will allow phased reductions in total public spending to be made.

That, in turn, will allow corresponding reductions in the overall burden of taxation. And that will help to meet the objection made to resource and pollution taxes that, if they are successful in reducing resource use and pollution, they will reduce their own base.

3.3. SUMMARY OF POLICY IMPLICATIONS

The following are among the aspects of taxation and public expenditure that call for attention.

- As the practical and conceptual implications of ecotaxation become more apparent, energy, land and other resource and environmental taxes will be seen as payments for values subtracted from the common pool. An energy tax at source will help to achieve many of the objectives of ecotaxation.
- A site-value tax on land will be one of these resource taxes. For a long time economists have commended it as the least distortionary tax of all. It has particular merit in the context of sustainability.
- The merit and practical feasibility of a Citizen's Income (or Basic Income), paid to all citizens in place of existing tax allowances and many social welfare benefits (and which would in time replace some other public spending too), are increasingly apparent.

A combination should be phased in over a period of years of:

- energy, land and environmental taxes,
- reductions in existing taxes on employment, incomes, profits, value-added and saving, and
- a Citizen's Income.

This would make it possible to avoid the otherwise regressive effects of ecotaxes, and the socially divisive and economically damaging effects of social benefits and taxes targeted at particular groups of people and businesses. It would also have the makings of a new social compact, appropriate to a sustainable economy in which full employment has become a thing of the past.

Public purchasing policies should encourage sustainable and equitable practices on the part of contractors, thus contributing to sustainable and equitable practices throughout the economy.

Systematic annual analyses should be published on the sustainability effects of all public subsidies (and related tax differentials and public expenditure), with a view to eliminating subsidies that favour unsustainable development.

Temporary subsidies for sustainable development initiatives such as green investment funds should be considered. But the elimination of the existing bias of taxation and public expenditure towards unsustainability is more important.

Systematic annual analyses should be published on the possibilities for re-orientating public spending programmes, with the aim of preventing and reducing environmental and social problems before the event, rather than concentrating on trying to clean up and remedy their effects after the event.

The developments discussed here on taxation and public expenditure will contribute to evolving a more people-centred economy. Enabling people to meet more of their needs for themselves and one another will make it possible, over time, to reduce total public spending. That, in turn, will allow reductions in the revenue required from taxation. Those will be aspects of the growth of the informal sector relatively to the formal sector, and of the decline in the government-centredness (and business-centredness) of today's economic system.

Notes

1 This book does not go into the merits of tradable pollution permits. If sold to businesses by government (as, in principle, they should be), tradable permits raise public revenue and provide incentives to reduce environmental impact, as ecotaxes do. But, as von Weizsacker (1994), pp146-147, points out, tradable permits have serious drawbacks as a general alternative to ecotaxes.
2 Mulgan and Murray (1993), pp36-39.
3 This book does not include a discussion of 'hypothecation', whereby the revenue from a particular tax or charge is earmarked for a particular purpose. As a general principle of taxation there are objections to hypothecation, but as a way of securing public support for a new tax there may be arguments for it (see O'Riordan (1997), pp37-59). (The systemic restructuring of taxation and public expenditure discussed here might possibly be seen as an instance of hypothecation on a grand scale. As will be seen, the use to be made of the revenue from the new taxes helps to remove one of the main objections to them.)
4 Ekins (1986) pp230-232.
5 For examples, see Annex B and Annex C.
6 David Richards, *The Land Value of Britain*, 1985-1990, Economic and Social Science Research Association.
7 Fred Harrison in Ronald Banks (ed) (1989).
8 Appendix to Richard Noyes (ed) (1991).
9 Mason Gaffney and Fred Harrison (1994).
10 Brittan, S. and Webb, S. (1990)
11 Clark, C. and Healy, J. (1997).
12 The British Government Panel on Sustainable Development (First Report, January 1995, para 16) supported a move toward taxing people *'on the value they subtract'* rather than *'the value they add'*.
13 DIW (1994).
14 von Weiszacker (1994), p76.

15 For the application of similar principles at the global level, combining taxes on nations' use of global 'commons' with the distribution of a global 'citizen's income', see section 5.3. 2.
16 UK Panel on Sustainable Development (1997), p11.
17 Ibid, p12.
18 The necessary existence of some such framework is one reason why a totally 'free' market, based on objectively 'true' prices, is a logical impossibility. See Chapter 6 for discussion of what this means for the status of economic measurement and analysis based on supposedly objective prices.

Chapter 4

Money and finance

'If money be not thy servant, it will be thy master.'

Pierre Charron (1601)

Most of the sectoral changes involved in the shift to sustainable development, summarized in Chapter 2, have been well worked through by NGOs, professional experts and others in recent years. The policy changes they call for in the spheres of taxation and public expenditure, discussed in Chapter 3, are moderately easy to understand. Not everyone agrees with them, and there will certainly be opposition to implementing them. But it is not too difficult to see how governments and government agencies could set about examining them in depth, with a view to converting them to detailed practical policy proposals, given the will and the policy-making capacity to do so.

In addition to changes in the pattern of government revenues and expenditures, sustainable development also calls for changes in the way the actual money and finance system works. The way it works at present encourages unsustainable development, and helps to create poverty and dependency for many people and places. This is increasingly recognized by NGOs and the new economics movement. Some specific developments in the sphere of monetary and financial institutions (such as LETS, local and social investment, and microcredit) are now part of the new economics agenda.[1] But money is conceptually more complex and more clouded in professional mystery than most other fields of policy. It has been difficult for policy makers in other fields, and for NGOs, to get to grips with it. Strategic understanding still has to crystallize about the changes implied by a shift to people-centred, sustainable development in the sphere of money and finance.

This section starts by outlining certain specific ways in which the workings of money and finance today cause damage to people and the environment. It notes that criticism of the way the system works is rising. It then considers the emergence of a post-modern perspective on money, and some of the questions it will increasingly raise. Against that background it discusses some specific issues that require attention. It concludes with a summary of policy implications. (International financial questions are dealt with in Chapter 5.)

4.1. DAMAGING EFFECTS

There are two main reasons why today's money and finance system is a powerful cause of unsustainable development.

- It systematically transfers resources from poor to rich.
- The money-must-grow imperative drives production (and therefore consumption and investment) to ever higher levels.

4.1.1. Transfer of resources from poor to rich

The transfer of resources from poor people to rich people, from poor places to rich places, and from poor countries to rich countries by the money and finance system is systematic. No one actually decides from time to time that this is a desired policy goal. It compels poor people and countries, and encourages rich ones, to consume resources and create pollution and waste faster than they would otherwise do. The poor have to do it to survive. The affluent, for whom economic survival offers no problem, enjoy the luxury to do it both in their leisure activities and in pursuit of further financial growth and success.

One cause of the transfer of wealth from poor *people* to rich is the way interest payments and receipts work through the economy. Dividing the population into ten sections of equal size, a German study (Kennedy 1995) suggested that the effect of interest is that the richest section receives far more than it pays, the second richest receives a little more, and the other eight receive less. The result is a substantial transfer of money from the poorer majority of the population to the rich minority.

The transfer of money from poorer to richer *localities* takes place through the automatic workings of the national and international banking and financial networks. Because poorer localities offer fewer attractive investment opportunities, savings from them are channelled into investments in richer parts of the country or richer parts of the world which offer better returns. This is quite natural. It reflects the service that the banking and financial system is expected to provide for savers and investors, and it is how it expects to make profits for itself. The same principle leads to the transfer of financial resources between poorer and richer countries.

The case of Third World debt in the 1980s and 1990s illustrates some of the causes and effects of the systematic transfer of wealth from poorer to richer *countries*. International interest rates rose and so did the cost of imported know-how and technologies, while international commodity prices fell. This was through no fault of indebted Third World countries. Nonetheless, they found themselves faced with escalating debts, in the form of interest to be paid and principal to be repaid, and with reduced foreign exchange earnings to pay them with.[2] The response of the International Monetary Fund and the World Bank was to prescribe development policies that placed even greater emphasis on the export of commodities (at low world prices) – requiring the indebted countries to achieve a foreign exchange surplus from which they could pay off their debts.

One result was to set back the process of building the capacity of those countries' national economies to meet the needs of their own peoples. A more immediate result was to create greater poverty and, consequently, greater stress on local environments. That, together with the need to step up the export of commodities to earn increased foreign exchange, accelerated the pace of environmentally damaging resource exploitation.

In the long term, the loan needs of Third World countries would be reduced if they received annual 'rental' or compensation payments in recognition of the disproportionately large use of world resources by the industrialized countries. More immediately, as a millennial commitment to sustainable world development, the unrepayable debts of the poorest countries should be cancelled. (For more on both these points see 5.3.)

4.1.2. Money must grow[3]

National Income must grow (for further discussion of GDP growth see Chapter 6), corporate profits and stockmarket values must grow, financial institutions profit from growth of the money supply and consumer credit, and individuals want their incomes and financial assets to grow. This money-must-grow imperative drives production (and therefore consumption and investment) to higher levels than would otherwise be needed.

One example is how the existence of interest and the discount rate tend to encourage more rapid exploitation of resources than would otherwise happen. Converting resources into a financial profit now, and saving or investing the profit, yields an annual return; whereas leaving the resources in the ground or the sea yields no annual return until they are extracted.

4.2. AN EMERGING POST-MODERN PERSPECTIVE

Those are some specific ways in which the workings of the money system now contribute to unsustainable development. They are already contributing to changes in people's perceptions of the money and finance system, and their attitudes towards it, which will be important for the future.

For example, it is becoming more widely recognized that the dominating role of money in late modern society parallels the role of religion in the late Middle Ages. Then the local church was the most prominent building in most villages; today the prime sites in every high street are occupied by branches of banks and other financial concerns. The centres of medieval cities were dominated by cathedrals; today's city centres are dominated by the tower blocks of international banks. Today's army of accountants, bankers, tax-people, insurance brokers, stock jobbers, foreign exchange dealers and countless other specialists in money is the modern counterpart of the medieval army of priests, friars, monks, nuns, abbots and abbesses, pardoners, summoners and other specialists in religious procedures and practices. The theologians of the late Middle Ages have their counterpart in the financial analysts and economists of the late industrial age.

At the time of the Protestant Reformation in 16th century Europe, the Church was experienced by increasing numbers of people as having lost its meaning, and being detached from real life, out of control, and grossly exploitative. Just so, the money and finance system is increasingly experienced around the world today as unreal, incomprehensible, unaccountable, exploitative, out of control. Why should people lose their houses and their jobs as a result of financial decisions taken in distant parts of the world? Why should the national and international money and finance system involve the systematic transfer of wealth from poor people to rich people, and from poor countries to rich countries? Why should someone in Singapore be able to gamble on the Tokyo stock exchange and bring about the collapse of a bank in London? Why, when taking out a pension, should people have had to rely on advice corrupted by the self-interest of the advisers? Why do young people trading derivatives in the City of London get annual bonuses larger than the whole annual budgets of primary schools? People are beginning to wonder if we have to have a money and financial system that works like this.

Worldwide public criticism of the way the money, banking and finance system works is growing and will continue to grow. Even George Soros now says ('Capital Crimes', *Atlantic Monthly*, January 1997) that 'the untrammelled intensification of *laisser-faire* capitalism and the extension of market values into all areas of life is endangering our open and democratic society. The main enemy of the open society, I believe, is no longer the communist but the capitalist threat'. Among the groups articulating concern about money, banking and finance are Bankwatch (a coalition of organizations co-ordinated by the New Economics Foundation) and the Institute for Financial Services and Consumer Protection (IFF) in Hamburg. While policy makers will have to continue to respond to particular financial scandals and crises as they occur, they also need to be aware of the longer-term concerns arising in the public mind. The following are among the questions likely to become increasingly pressing.

4.2.1. What is money for?

What functions do we need the money and finance system to perform? What is it supposed to be for? The answer, surely, must be that we need it to support our economic activities – to help us to engage in economic transactions that benefit one another, and to provide ourselves and one another with a degree of economic security for the future. How money and finance do this, or should do it, is becoming clearer with the arrival of the Information Age.

Over the centuries, money has evolved from concrete to abstract – from metal bars and coins, to paper notes and cheques, and now to numbers electronically stored in computer files and transmitted electronically between them. As this stage has arrived – with the transformation of the great majority of monetary and financial assets and liabilities into entries in computerized accounts, and of the great majority of monetary and financial transactions into electronic messages that debit and credit the accounts of payer and payee – our collective understanding of money and its role in economic life is reaching a watershed. It is becoming increasingly apparent that the money and finance system is basically an information system – an accounting system (or scoring system) that indicates the claims we are entitled to make on one another for goods and services now and in the future, and enables us to trade one type of claim (e.g. money in a bank account) for another type of claim (e.g. an insurance policy or a shareholding in a business).

4.2.2. Should money reflect objective values?

Historically, money was provided for society – it was often imposed on it – by priests and kings and governments. Our historical experience of it was of something external to us, not ours to understand or question. Adam Smith's view that money numbers should as nearly as possible reflect 'real prices' (just as in modern science numerical data are expected to reflect objective facts in the 'real world'), lingers on into the late modern age. The suggestion still put forward from time to time that a currency should be linked to the market value of a basket of basic commodities (grain, oil, etc) expresses this modern hankering for external objectivity.

But the post-modern perception of the world – hitherto most clearly articulated in literature and the arts – is more subjective. To an important extent, we create our own pluralistic realities. In the post-modern world, therefore, money will come to be perceived as no more than an institutional instrument, to be further developed by people for people's purposes. The idea that there should be only one kind of money at national level or even European or eventually even global level – a single currency that everyone should be compelled to use – may come to seem archaic. The notion that monetary and banking experts – like a priesthood or scientific elite whose arcane methods people cannot hope to understand – should be entrusted with the task of keeping money values in line with mysteriously existing objective numerical realities out there, will probably seem primitive. The perception will no doubt spread that a unit of money has no intrinsic value of its own, and need have none as long as it works well for the task that people need it to perform.

4.2.3. Whose money system is it?

Who does the money system belong to? It is not clear how most people in Europe would answer this question today. But in some years' time, surely, most will say that it belongs to us, the people, collectively. We need it as a common facility or resource that will enable us to carry out economic transactions with each other.

In this context Local Exchange Trading Systems (LETS), though in practice still very marginal, embody a potentially important model for the future – the perception of a money system as essentially something we can create for ourselves to facilitate exchanges between us. Although we need someone to manage the system for us, the system is ours to be managed on our collective behalf.[4]

Perceiving the money system as a common facility or resource suggests that we should pay for it according to the use we make of it. As rich people make greater use of money than poor, they would pay more. (This possibility is noted again at 4.3.2. below.)

4.2.4. Why does the system work badly?

Once this question is asked, the answer becomes fairly clear. The primary interest of the goldsmiths and bankers and government servants who have evolved the monetary, banking and financial system over the centuries, and the primary interest of the great majority of the bankers and other financial specialists who manage it today, has been to make money for their customers, shareholders and other associates, and for themselves and their own organizations. Nobody has ever been responsible for ensuring that the monetary and financial system's prime function is to work efficiently and fairly for all its users – locally, nationally and worldwide. It has never been designed for that purpose. Economists and financial analysts have never been employed to work out what might be involved in designing it and managing it with that in view.

With the arrival of the Information Age, pressure will grow to work out how the money system should evolve, and how it should be managed, if it is to perform efficiently and fairly the functions we require of it. In the context of sustainable development, the challenge for policy makers is to make sure that the money system evolves as an accounting (or scoring) system, which will operate to serve common interests, and the interests of all its users – locally, nationally and globally.

4.3. CURRENCIES, INTEREST AND DEBT

4.3.1. A single or multiple currency system?

The proposal for a single European currency is a very live issue at the present time. What is said here is unlikely to affect the policy positions taken on it for the time being. But policy makers with an eye to the future may recognize its relevance to the situation that will develop, either after a single currency has been adopted by a number of countries of the European Union, or after the introduction of a single currency has been delayed.

Compelling everyone to use a particular currency is in line with the well-established historical impulse to centralize economic power and decision making. As Jane Jacobs (1984) put it, 'Today we take it for granted that the elimination of multitudinous currencies in favour of fewer national or imperial currencies represents economic progress and promotes the stability of economic life. But this conventional belief is still worth questioning . . . National or imperial currencies give faulty or destructive feedback to city economies and this in turn leads to profound structural flaws in those economies, some of which cannot be overcome, however hard we try.'

In fact, not only urban local economies suffer. Rural local economies confront the same problem. When local economies, urban or rural, have to depend on national (or supranational) currencies as the medium of exchange to facilitate economic activity within their own local boundaries, declining local ability to compete in the national and international economy results in too little money coming into local circulation even to support entirely local transactions. Local unemployment then rises, local land and other physical assets lie unused, and local needs remain unmet – all for want of enough money circulating locally to facilitate local exchange. The monetary policies and demand management policies appropriate for a national (or continental) economy at any particular time are bound to be inappropriate for many of the local economies within it. More flexibility is needed. The pressures of globalization are accentuating the problem for many local economies.

Significant pointers to the future include a growing number of local currencies or quasi-currencies (including LETS). Interest continues to grow in the currency experiments of Austrian local government authorities in the 1930s, which successfully reduced local unemployment until they were suppressed by the Austrian government and central bank. The amount of useful literature on local currencies is mounting steadily. (See Greco 1994, Douthwaite 1996, and the references they quote.) (The rather different idea of a 'twin economy' with its own twin currency, operating in the spheres of the informal economy and community exchange systems in parallel with the formal economy, has also been suggested – *Demos* 2/1994).

The underlying question is whether the simultaneous move towards greater globalization and greater localization of economic decision making will, and should, be accompanied by the emergence of both supranational and local currencies. This would seem to be a logical possibility, looking to the longer term. It would be in keeping with the subsidiarity principle. It would imply organic development towards a multi-level European system of currencies, with:

- a new *common* (not single) European currency,
- existing national currencies,
- optional new local currencies, quasi-currencies and media of exchange, issued by local government authorities which chose to issue them, and
- optional neighbourhood and community quasi-currencies and media of exchange, on the lines of LETS.

The keynote would be freedom of choice, not compulsion. Local government authorities and local neighbourhood and community groups would have the option to introduce their own means of exchange if they thought it useful to do so. People and organizations would have the freedom to agree with one another to use whichever currency they thought most appropriate and convenient for their transaction. Banks and other financial service providers could operate accounts for their customers denominated in the different currencies.

Virtually no serious study has yet been carried out by monetary authorities or monetary economists on how a multi-level currency system on these lines would work, and in particular how relations between the different currencies might be expected to develop.

> *'Evaluating the implications of multiple and, particularly, comple-mentary currency systems . . . is practically a virgin academic field.'*

> (Lietaer 1996)

Might some currencies drive others out? Might they have infla-tionary effects? If so, how could those be prevented? Would currency exchanges be regulated? Would they be taxed? If so, how? Would national and local governments (and the European Commission) insist that whenever possible their own currencies should be used in payments to and from themselves? Which currency would be used for payments between different levels of government?

Proactive contingency planning requires study of these and other questions to be put in hand, to explore – with the aid of computer modelling – possible problems that evolution towards a multi-level currency system may throw up, and possible responses to them.

4.3.2. Interest and currencies

The part played by interest in the transfer of money from poor to rich, and in the acceleration of resource extraction and environ-mental damage, has been mentioned above. So has the fact that the increasingly popular LETS involve no interest payments. But the question of interest is attracting increasing attention in a number of other ways too.

It has been asked for many years, in North America as well as in Europe, why the process of *issuing new money* into the economy (i.e. credit creation) is delegated by governments to the banking system, which issues it to bank customers in the form of interest-bearing loans. Why should the banks and their shareholders profit from the interest, and not the country's citizens? Should not governments (on their citizens' behalf) take back the ancient right of seignorage, and limit the banks to lending only money that had already been deposited with them? Over the years this question has been kept alive by successors to the Social Credit movement and others on the margins, and is now attracting new attention. For example, would an alternative way to issue new money, as required in accordance with monetary policy, be for governments to distribute it in equal amounts to all citizens as a component of a Citizens' Income?

However, that change in the process of creating new money might be only one aspect of a much more far-reaching set of proposals to *convert debt into equity* throughout the economy. This would be in line with Islamic teaching, and indeed with earlier Christian teaching, that usury is a sin. Having spent five years directing banking research, I have thought in the past that the idea was so 'politically unrealistic' that for practical purposes it could be ignored. But now I am not so sure. The role which debt now plays throughout the national and international economy, the contribution it makes to unsustainable development, the extent to which economic life is now trapped in and depends on rising debt, and the economic power this gives to institutions devoted to making money out of money rather than out of risk-bearing participation in real-life projects and enterprises, all demand keen examination. (Tomlinson 1993 and Kennedy 1995 provide good starting points.)

Negative interest rates or circulation fees were proposed earlier this century by Silvio Gesell (from whom Keynes said the future would learn more than from Marx). The principle was adopted in the Austrian local currency experiments noted above, requiring each currency note to be revalidated every month by attaching a special stamp to it costing 2 per cent of its value. The purpose was to speed up local circulation by encouraging people to spend, not hoard, the local money. (That type of circulation fee can be applied most easily to notes and coins. Applying the principle more generally would mean applying it to other liquid financial assets too.)

Note that *circulation fees* (or demurrage charges) are also a way of making users pay for the service of being provided with money.

As the principle underlying resource taxation becomes more widely established – that people should pay for the use they make of 'the commons' – and as that principle is extended to the use of common resources and facilities provided by society as well as by nature, the idea that people should pay for the use they make of the money system will come to seem quite logical. Another form of such payment would be a 'Tobin' tax on exchange transactions between one currency and another (see 5.3.2 below).

Note also that, if negative interest rates and demurrage charges became the norm, *discount rates* would become negative. Not only would equity investments generally become more attractive than bank deposits and other forms of liquidity, but investing in sustainable development for the long-term future would become more attractive too.

4.3.3. Electronic money and deregulation

Government authorities – local, national and supranational – may have less direct responsibility for the money system in the 21st century. Although privatizing it would not necessarily contribute to sustainable development, it seems likely that increasing numbers of commercial companies and community groups (e.g. LETS) will issue their own media of exchange in the coming years.

This could be an unplanned process of piecemeal development. But it is also possible that a free money movement comparable to the 19th-century free trade movement may emerge. Hayek (1978) foresaw this possibility over twenty years ago. Arguing that the government monopoly of money has been the cause of inflation, financial instability, undisciplined public expenditure and economic nationalism, he suggested its replacement by competition in currency supplied by private issuers. He also suggested that 'it will be through the credit card rather than through any kind of circulating token money that the government monopoly of the issue of money will be broken'.

The potential importance of electronic and plastic money is now widely recognized, including the prospect of rechargeable cash cards and money transmission over the Internet. At the same time, increasing numbers of retailers are launching their own credit cards and other financial services. The implications of this for policy making, for sustainable development and in other spheres, are not yet clear. But it needs to be recognized as part of the context in which new economic policies for sustainable development will have to be introduced.

4.4. FINANCIAL INSTITUTIONS

4.4.1. Conventional financial institutions

Towards sustainable survival and success

Constructive efforts are being made, and are likely to grow, to persuade financial institutions (such as insurance companies) that sustainable development is coming and that they should adjust their business strategies to it. In December 1996 an Oxford Solar Investment Summit organized by Greenpeace brought together eighty senior people from the financial services industry, the energy industry and the retail sector to discuss the linked environmental, industrial and investment opportunities offered by solar energy.[5] By 1996, ninety commercial banks from twenty-seven countries had signed the UN Environment Programme's (UNEP) Statement by Banks on Environment and Sustainable Development. Government policy should encourage these efforts. The most effective way of doing so will be through the changes in taxation and public spending discussed in Chapter 3. But other possible measures, such as short-term subsidies or tax-breaks for green investment (4.4.2 below), should be considered.

Sustainability auditing

It will be particularly important to apply to banks and other financial institutions the accounting, audit and accreditation procedures being developed to help and require business corporations to monitor and publish information about their impacts on sustainability. The social and ecological 'footprints' of financial institutions are not so direct or immediately obvious as those of other large corporations, but are often more far-reaching. 'The decisions of fund managers impact on the other side of the world. The rainforest may be geographically located in the Far East, but financially, as the benefits go to shareholders elsewhere, it might as well be in London's square mile' (*Creating a Sustainable London* 1996 – see Annex C, 2.5).

Legislative framework

It is for consideration whether a new legislative framework is needed for banks and other financial institutions that will balance their privileges with their obligations to society in the context of sustainable development.

4.4.2. New financial institutions

New types of financial institutions are evolving to meet the needs of people-centred sustainable development. These include:

- ethical, green and social banks, investment funds and financial advisory firms which cater for people who wish to put their savings and investments to what they regard as good use; and
- local development banks and microcredit banks and other grass-roots people's banks (new credit unions are also included) which provide credit for people and localities too poor to get it from conventional financial institutions.

Green and social investment

The conventional attitude to saving and investment has been that people's only concern should be to get 'value for money' for themselves. That is what conventional financial institutions and advisers have been in business to help people to do. But increasing numbers of people recognize that money brings power and responsibility. How we invest it helps to shape the future of society and the world, by channelling resources in certain directions instead of others. By using our money in accordance with our values, we can help in however small a way to shape the kind of society and the kind of world – more people-centred and sustainable – that we would like to see.[6]

How can government policies most effectively help people to use their savings as investors (and their spending power as consumers) to support sustainable development?

- The proposals in 2.7 for labelling ethical and green products and accrediting ethical and green companies will help, by improving the information that purposeful investors (and consumers) need.[7]
- The changes in taxation and public expenditure (Chapter 3) will help more than anything else, by creating an overall structure of prices that will favour sustainable investment (and sustainable forms of consumption – and less consumption). Without those changes, no amount of exhortation, information and guidance is likely to persuade more than a small minority of savers to invest in sustainable development at a financial cost to themselves.
- As a short-term temporary measure, special subsidies or tax breaks to encourage green investing may be justified. In January 1995 the Netherlands introduced a scheme enabling investors to invest tax-free in green investment funds.[8] But once the proposed changes in the structures of taxation and public spending begin to affect the overall structure of prices, subsidies should become unnecessary.

Local banking and microcredit institutions

Several different types of 'community banks' have been growing in numbers in North America and Europe and in countries of the South in recent years. They are set up to provide loans and other financial services to localities or groups of people (e.g. poor self-employed women in countries of the South) who are not served by conventional financial institutions. They include the following:[9]

- Community development banks, which provide loans and other financial services to particular localities. Examples are the South Shore Bank in Chicago, and the new Aston Redevelopment Trust in Birmingham, England.
- Community development loan funds, which provide loans primarily for co-operatives, community businesses and other social-economy enterprises. The Local Investment Fund (LIF) in the UK is an example.
- Credit Unions.
- Microloan or Microcredit Banks. The best known of these is the Grameen Bank in Bangladesh, which has provided a model for similar institutions in other countries. They organize small supportive groups of (mainly) women to save and borrow money in amounts which, though small, enable them to start or expand their own small enterprises.

These local banking and microcredit institutions have a key part to play in reviving many local economies now in decline and enabling many people now unemployed to generate work for themselves and others. Public policy should support them.

4.5. SUMMARY OF POLICY IMPLICATIONS

For good or ill, changes in the system of money and finance will play an important part in the shift towards sustainable development. Policy makers will have to come to terms with the issues this raises.

Awareness will grow of the unsustainable effects of the way the money and finance system works today. So will criticism of its unaccountable and exploitative nature. Questions will become more pressing about:

- what the money and finance system is for (what functions it is supposed to perform);
- who it is supposed to be for (who it belongs to);
- why it now systematically transfers wealth from the poor to the rich, and systematically encourages unsustainable development;
- how it can be designed to work better; and
- what a post-modern money and finance system will be like.

More specific issues cover:

- the possible emergence of multiple and multi-level currencies;
- proposals to mitigate the unsustainable effects of interest and debt;
- prospects for deregulated currencies and quasi-currencies;
- possible implications of electronic money;
- the need to apply sustainability accounting, auditing and accreditation procedures to financial institutions; and
- the role of green and social investment, and the role of local banking and microcredit institutions, in the shift to sustainability.

Notes

1 See 4.2.3 and 4.4.2 below for further discussion of LETS, local investment, social investment, and microcredit. See Annex B and Annex C for relevant organizations and publications.
2 Out of the $1,200 billion owed by the Third World to the First

World in 1990, only $400bn constituted the original borrowing. The rest consisted of accrued interest and capital liabilities. Brown (1993), p43.

3 Hoogendijk (1991 and subsequent papers) explores this problem.

4 A LETS is set up by a local community group of up to 250 members to provide a system of accounts in respect of transactions between them. The account of each member is held centrally by someone who manages the system. A new account starts at zero. As members carry out transactions with one another, they ask the central office to debit and credit their accounts with the number of units they have agreed. The system as a whole is always exactly balanced, with the total debit balances of members in debt being exactly matched by the total credit balances of members in credit. No interest is paid on debts. For more detailed discussion, see Douthwaite (1996), pp64ff.

5 Reported in *Greenpeace Business*, February/March 1997.

6 The ethical, green and social (e.g. fair trade – see 5.3.1) consumer movement also continues to grow, in spite of some scepticism in recent years about business approaches to green marketing. It parallels the ethical, etc, investment movement in several ways: in its aim to enable people to use their money (in this case purchasing money) purposefully; in moving away from the conventional consumer movement's concentration on helping consumers to get 'value for money' for themselves; and in the emergence of new initiatives to help consumers to consume more sustainably and ethically. For example, the international charity Global Action Plan (GAP) helps individuals to take positive and practical environmental action as consumers, workers and members of their communities.

7 Consumers also need guidance on how to understand their own 'ecological footprints' and how to reduce them by buying sustainable products and disposing of waste in sustainable ways (e.g. whenever possible, for repairing, reconditioning, recycling or re-use).

8 I owe this information to Triodos Bank. The responsible government department is the Ministry of Housing, Spatial Planning and the Environment, P.O.Box 30945, 2500 GX The Hague.

9 A useful short summary is in *New Economics*, Issue 37, Spring 1996.

Chapter 5

The global economy

'I sympathise, therefore, with those who would minimise, rather than with those who would maximise, economic entanglement between nations. Ideas, knowledge, art, hospitality, travel – these are the things which should of their nature be international. But let goods be homespun whenever it is reasonably and conveniently possible; and, above all, let finance be primarily national.'

J.M. Keynes (1933)[1]

It will be in the interest of Europeans that European policy makers (at national and European levels) play a full part in the evolution of global governance, for a 21st-century world in which the European and North American hegemony of the past few centuries will be in relative decline. This chapter outlines policy approaches that could help to shape more effective and more democratic global economic policies and institutions. These will be needed to promote the necessary worldwide shift to a new path of development that is people-centred and environmentally sustainable.

It will involve reversing a central feature of world economic development hitherto – the relatively higher rate of growth of international trade and, to an even greater extent, of international financial flows, than of world economic output. In that regard, the new economics perception accords with Keynes' well-known statement quoted above.

5.1. THE GLOBAL CONTEXT AND EUROPE'S ROLE

Two great changes can be foreseen in the next half-century – one in the structure of world power and the other in the nature of the world's economic progress.

As regards the structure of power, the modern period of history – the past 500 years – has been one of European and North American world domination, economically and politically. In the 21st century that supremacy will decline. The balance of economic power is already shifting. Japan and South East Asia are competitive now. China, India, Indonesia and Brazil soon will be. As time passes, the balance of geopolitical power will shift too. Meanwhile, the capacity of national governments to exercise sovereign power will continue to decline, in response to globalization and localization. These changes present a challenge to democracy. They call for the development of more democratic institutions at global and local levels, as well as the national (and European) level. They also require democratic institutions to extend their reach over the economic dimension.

The growing importance of international NGOs and citizens' movements is relevant. They are playing an increasingly prominent part in international discussions about developments in the global economy, including changes needed in organizations like the World Bank, International Monetary Fund (IMF) and General Agreement on Tariffs and Trade (GATT)/World Trade Organisation (WTO).[2] They are closely linked with NGOs, citizens' movements and third-sector socio-economic enterprises and initiatives in the national economies of both North and South. They represent a growing force in global economic decision making. Most of them are committed to local self-reliant, sustainable development.

As regards economic progress, it cannot continue for long in its present form. That is widely understood, and is what this book is about. The existing human population is already consuming

112

and polluting more than Earth can sustain. Ultimately world population may double. It could never be possible for all people on Earth to attain the high-consuming, high-polluting ways of life of today's rich countries, although Western business communications media and Western business marketing, supported by Western governments, continue to promote them worldwide. A change in the direction of progress is bound to come. It will come either by a deliberate shift to sustainable development or as the aftermath of catastrophic global breakdown – or a mixture of the two.

To avoid catastrophe and to shift in good order to a sustainable development path, the world community will need to act on an agreed global compact on the following lines.

- The rich North will shift to a new conserving and empowering development path, as outlined in earlier sections. It will involve more efficient use of a smaller share of the world's natural resources (which we now overuse), and more efficient use of our human resources (which we now underemploy and under-develop).
- The 'developing' countries of the South and the countries of the former Soviet bloc will also switch to this conserving and empowering development path.[3] In our own self-interest we in the North will do all we can to help the South and the former Soviet bloc countries to shift to this new path of progress.
- Changes will be made in today's global patterns of trade, investment and aid, and in existing ways of regulating them, which will support equitable and sustainable development. The institutions of global economic governance will be brought under more democratic control. At present the World Bank, IMF and WTO do not represent or answer to the majority of the world's governments, let alone the world's peoples, and do not have their confidence.

The North has already lost the power to *compel* the peoples of the majority world (who now consume and pollute much less than we do) to adopt this new path of more conserving and more self-reliant progress. Unless we can persuade them to do so by negotiating a compact on the lines above, their further development may seriously damage our future.

In short, the peoples and governments of Europe should aim to make a threefold contribution to global development in the coming years:

- show that we are committed to reorienting our own way of life towards sustainable development;
- ensure that our own national and European activities in the spheres of international trade, investment and aid contribute to sustainable, not unsustainable, development in other parts of the world; and
- participate effectively with the rest of the international community in the building of new global policies and institutions in support of sustainable and equitable development.

Previous chapters have been about the policies implied by the first of these three points.

5.2. UNILATERAL NATIONAL (AND EUROPEAN) POLICIES

The policy proposals covered in previous sections would have some benign spillover effects on sustainable development in other parts of the world. But there is also scope for policy changes specifically aimed at contributing to it. It will involve reviewing existing policies and programmes on

- export promotion,
- outward investment,

- aid and technology transfer, and
- trade,

to make sure they do not contribute to unsustainable development in recipient countries or elsewhere.

A government seriously committed to sustainable development will examine how far, for example, its support for arms exports contributes to unsustainability. That is one of the controversial questions that arises. More generally, governments should undertake systematic annual reviews of the extent to which their export promotion, outward investment, aid and technology transfer policies could be reoriented towards sustainable development. Many desirable policy changes would be identified. For example, governments should 'publish guidelines which set out the environmental standards which transfer of technology should meet, and a list of technologies which should not be transferred' (British Government Panel on Sustainable Development 1995, p17). And increased government support could be given to 'fair trade' (see 5.3.1, p 117).

A similarly systematic approach is called for at the European level too. As mentioned already (section 2.1), one aim of changes in the Common Agricultural Policy should be to encourage more sustainable agriculture in Third World countries as well as in Europe. The Wuppertal Institute's 1995 study on Sustainable Germany found that the European Union's relations with the countries of the South 'are determined by two disparate, uncoordinated and therefore contradictory tendencies. On the one hand they are protected by trade agreements, particularly in the case of those countries that are linked to the EU by their colonial past. But the EU also protects its market and trade interests with measures which damage the very countries it wishes to support with its development cooperation. This is done by import restrictions and export subsidies'.[4] The European Sustainable Development Initiative (ESDI) for European development cooperation, which was proposed by WWF in January 1997, reflects the need for more active co-ordination of all the various departmental and other interests involved.[5]

5.3. CREATING A GLOBAL FRAMEWORK

The UN system, together with the World Bank, IMF and GATT/WTO does not, in its existing form, provide an effective framework of policies and institutions for sustainable global development. Because the World Bank, IMF and GATT/WTO (or whatever successor institutions take their place in the coming years) will play such a key role in global economic cooperation and development in the 21st century, particular attention should be paid to criticisms of their policies – and of their position within the UN system.

It is now widely agreed that their policies have damaged – 'developed to death' – the livelihoods and environments of many of the world's peoples, and will continue to do so unless they are changed more radically than is now proposed. Reflecting orthodox economic principles and conventional economic philosophy, they have imposed forms of development based on externally financed mega-projects, export-led growth and 'free' trade. This has reinforced the vulnerability of many countries in the South to external economic factors beyond their control, such as low export prices and high world interest rates.

In many cases the resulting financial pressures, including the pressure to earn foreign currency to repay their escalating debt, have led directly to environmentally damaging exploitation of these countries' natural resources, including tropical forests. The poverty that results from this model of development and now afflicts well over a billion people, leads to further ecological degradation – besides being intolerable in itself.

5.3.1. Trade

'The highly integrated global economy of the 1990s, dominated by the activities of a few hundred transnational corporations, bears little relation to the economic configuration of the post-war 1940s in which the GATT rules were conceived, nor to the models of perfect competition which justified their emphasis on free trade. All but the most committed proponents of the free market recognise that efficient markets need effective government frameworks. Yet such a framework at the international level does not exist.'

(Ekins 1993)

One of the most controversial aspects of globalization has been and continues to be the development under the auspices of GATT/WTO of a global trading regime supposedly based on free trade. The fact that free trade has not applied to the large proportion of world trade between the subsidiaries of trans-national corporations or to sectors, such as food and agriculture, where the rich countries have thought their interests better served by a world market managed by themselves, makes it no less controversial. In reality, of course, there never has been and never could be totally free trade. Some participants in the international market place are always so much more powerful than others that, without regulation, the freedom of the latter will suffer. That was recognized in the old imperial dictum: 'trade follows the flag, and the flag follows trade'.[6]

In recent years rising hostility to free trade has taken a variety of forms. These include strenuous opposition to the North American Free Trade Area (NAFTA). There have been many calls for a 'new protectionism' (e.g. Lang and Hines 1993). There have been others for 'fair trade' (e.g. Brown 1993).

World Bank economists Daly and Goodland (in a personal capacity, 1993) are among many who have shown that unregulated free trade is damaging to the environment and to the development prospects of poorer countries. It has also been demonstrated (e.g.

by Daly and Cobb 1989 and Ekins 1995) that the classical 'comparative advantage' argument in support of unregulated free trade only applies in special hypothetical conditions which do not now exist (if they ever did) – e.g. when all the costs of production and distribution, including environmental and social costs, are internalized in product prices; and when factors of production are immobile, so that neither capital nor labour is able to flow across national boundaries.[7]

However, the prospect of a backlash in favour of conventional protectionism, with national governments unilaterally raising tariff and non-tariff barriers against imports from countries alleged to be guilty of environmental and social dumping, would be hardly less alarming than the prospect of unregulated free trade. In practice, protectionist policies damage the national economic performance of the protectionist country, because they almost always operate in favour of well-established national monopolies and power groups. By triggering tit-for-tat responses from other countries, they damage the wider common interest too.

To sum up, 'one of the early priorities of the WTO will be to ensure that action can be taken to protect the global environment in a way compatible with the principles of non-discrimination and transparency, and not as a cover for protectionism' (Commission on Global Governance (1995), p170). What is needed is an international framework of regulation that will apply uniformly to all countries and so give all the same degree of trading freedom, but will also be designed to encourage the types of trade that contribute to self-reliant, sustainable development rather than to dependency-creating, unsustainable growth.

Fair trade

The primary aim of the fair trading or alternative trading movement has been to link concerned consumers in the North with small producers in the South, and enable them to trade on a basis of fairness and mutual understanding. The driving force

118

behind it has come from charities and NGOs concerned with Third World development, such as (in the UK) Oxfam, CIIR (Catholic Institute for International Relations) and Christian Aid. Some alternative trading enterprises, such as Cafedirect, have become quite well known.

The fair trading movement has close links with the ethical consumer and ethical investment movements (see Chapter 4). They have many common supporters. As the NGOs concerned have begun to develop methods of monitoring the social and environmental performance of the producer organizations, this has enabled them to help – and bring pressure on – large commercial companies to do the same with their suppliers and contractors in the South (NEF/CIIR 1997). This is a significant aspect of corporate social and environmental accounting, auditing and reporting. (See 2.7.)

NGO and citizen support for fair trade seems almost certain to grow. It clearly has a contribution to make to sustainable development. It should attract favourable interest and, eventually, active support from governments and the WTO.

5.3.2. Finance

Third World debt

> 'The position for many low-income debtors – involving mainly debt owed to governments and official agencies – is still desperate despite repeated initiatives to write off a sizeable chunk of their debt. More than twenty African countries have debt burdens regarded by the World Bank as unsustainable.'

(Commission on Global Governance (1995), p201.)

There is a strong case for European governments and banks (and other governments and banks in the North) to cancel the unrepayable debts of the poorest countries. This could be done in advance of the Millennium, as an indication of commitment

119

to a global strategy for sustainable development in the 21st century.

Global taxation

> '*A start must be made in establishing schemes of financing of global purposes, including charges for the use of global resources such as flight lanes, sea lanes, and ocean fishing areas, and the collection of global revenues agreed globally and implemented by treaty. An international tax on foreign currency transactions should be explored as one option, as should the creation of an international corporate tax base among multinational companies. It is time for the evolution of a consensus on the concept of global taxation for servicing the needs of the global neighbourhood.'*

(Commission on Global Governance (1995), p344.)

Many proposals have been put forward in recent years for funding the United Nations and other institutions of global governance. On the principle of 'no taxation without representation', the eventual decisions will have implications for the democratization of the UN. If financial contributions to the UN continue to be based on the wealth and national incomes of member nations, questions will continue to arise about how to balance the rights of wealthy nations in recognition of their larger financial contributions, against the rights of the not-so-wealthy majority to have their interests fairly represented in the decision-making process. That issue could be avoided, at least to some extent, if the taxes and charges raised were of types that reflected the demands that each nation makes on 'global commons' – i.e. its use of common world resources, including the global capacity to absorb pollution and waste.[8]

Among possible global taxes that might meet this criterion (see Bezanson and Mendez in *Futures* 27/2, 1995) are:

- taxes and charges on use of international resources such as ocean fishing, sea-bed mining, sea lanes, flight lanes, outer space, and the electro-magnetic spectrum;
- taxes and charges on activities that pollute and damage the global environment, or that cause hazards across (or outside) national boundaries, such as emissions of CO_2 and CFCs, oil spills, dumping wastes at sea, and other forms of marine and air pollution;
- a tax on military expenditures and the arms trade;
- a more general tax on world trade, designed both to raise international revenue and also to give a uniform worldwide incentive to greater national economic self-reliance; and
- a uniform tax on international currency exchange transactions.[9]

Chapter 3 discussed the possibility of restructuring national taxes and welfare benefits so as to combine taxes on the use of common resources with the distribution of a Citizen's Income. The introduction of global taxes of the types listed above would provide an opportunity to apply the same principle at the global level. Nations would be charged according to their use of world resources, including their use of the capacity of the global environment to absorb pollution and wastes. The revenue would accrue to a fund at UN level, though perhaps operationally independent of the UN itself. A proportion of the revenue would be distributed to all nations according to the size of their populations, reflecting the right of every person in the world to a 'global citizen's income' based on an equal share of the value of global resources. The rest of the revenue could be used to finance UN expenditures, including international peacekeeping programmes.

This approach would:

- encourage sustainable development worldwide;
- generate a needed source of revenue for the UN;

- provide substantial financial transfers which developing countries would receive, by right and without strings, as 'rent' payments from the high-consuming, high-polluting, rich industrial countries for their disproportionate use of world resources; and
- help to liberate developing countries from their present degree of dependence on aid and on rich-country-dominated institutions such as the World Bank and the International Monetary Fund.

Towards a global currency?

As the Commission on Global Governance (1995) pointed out (pp179ff), the international monetary and financial system suffers from a number of weaknesses. The causes of the system's instability include:

- the globalization of private financial markets,
- huge international financial flows which far exceed trade in their impacts on currency markets,
- the fact that the IMF's reserve currency – Special Drawing Rights (SDRs) – currently accounts for only a very minor part of world liquidity, and
- the fact that 'the United States has the unique luxury of being able to borrow its own currency abroad and then devalue its repayment obligations' (p181).

'There are important tasks to be performed by the IMF or any other custodian of the international financial system, and these are growing in urgency' (p183).

As it comes to be accepted that there is a global economy to be managed and that it must be managed sustainably, one possibility would be to move towards a global currency by developing SDRs as a world unit of account for use by the UN and others (e.g.

transnational corporations) who would find it convenient. SDRs might evolve in time into a common (but not a single!) world currency. They might be issued annually in the form of a per capita distribution to all national governments, and in the form of credits (through the World Bank) for development aid, by an organization (which might be seen as an embryonic world central bank) combining the existing functions of the IMF and the Bank for International Settlements. Another suggestion (Lietaer 1996), is that a 'Global Reference Currency' might take the form of a demurrage currency, which would be subject to negative interest for as long as it remained in circulation. (See 4.3.2.)

These, as yet, are no more than possibilities. But the international monetary and financial system needs to, and will, evolve further in one way or another in the next few years. It will be important that its evolution takes full account of the need to shift to a new path of people-centred sustainable global development. This is an aim which European policy makers should seek to support.

5.3.3. Restructuring global institutions

The first half of the 1990s, leading up to the 50th anniversary of the UN and Bretton Woods (World Bank, IMF and GATT) institutions in 1995/96, saw growing awareness that the system of global governance set up after the 2nd World War would have to be restructured. Changes in the world since 1945, and particularly since the end of the Cold War, meant that the tasks of these institutions now were very different from those for which they had originally been designed.

Growing concern for sustainable development, before and after the UN Conference on Environment and Development (UNCED or Earth Summit) in Rio de Janeiro in 1992, was one important factor. Another was the need to reform the Security Council in order to reflect the changing balance of world population and geopolitical power. There were calls to formalize the growing participation of citizens' movements and NGOs along-side the officials of national governments formally represented in the UN and Bretton Woods institutions.[10] More generally, an urgent need for more effective co-ordination between different parts of the UN system and, in particular, between the UN system itself and the Bretton Woods institutions, was widely recognized.

On that last point, it was as long ago as 1990 that Sir Brian Urquhart and the late Erskine Childers, both recently retired from high-level posts in the UN, publicly doubted whether the UN's tasks could be carried out effectively 'until the work of the IMF, the World Bank and the GATT is conducted in harmony and cooperation with the rest of the UN system'.[11] In 1991 the Stockholm Initiative (which led to the setting up of the Commission on Global Governance) supported the proposal 'that the International Monetary Fund and the World Bank be coordinated, among themselves and with the United Nations system and GATT, with the aim of a clearer division of labour, better harmony and full universality in their work'.[12] Discussions at UNCED in 1992 on the need to evolve and implement a global strategy for sustainable development, and the establishment of a new Commission on Sustainable Development (CSD) in the UN, and a new Global Environment Facility (GEF) of the World Bank, underlined the importance of that proposal. It still remains to be implemented.

The detachment of the World Bank, IMF and GATT/WTO from the rest of the UN system reflects the dominating position of the Group of Seven (G7) rich industrial countries, in financing and shaping the activities of those institutions and in the world economy more generally.[13]

At their 1990 Economic Summit at Houston, the G7 leaders declared that the 1990s would be 'the Decade of Democracy'. This declaration has not yet been taken seriously in the economic sphere. The comparative failure of UNCED and of follow-up action in the five years since 1992 demonstrates the need for

124

more effective global economic institutions. To be effective, they must be more democratic; they must enjoy the confidence of the South as well as the North in the negotiation and management of 'our common future'. When sustainable development is the goal, it makes questionable sense for patterns of world development, trade and finance to continue to be dominated by rich, high-consumption, high-pollution countries like the USA, Germany, Japan, Britain, France, Canada and Italy, and for that particular group of countries to maintain disproportionate influence over the management and policies of the institutions of global economic governance.

How can the G7 Summits now begin to evolve into a more representative form of World Economic Council? How will such a World Economic Council fit in with other parts of the UN system, such as the Security Council, the General Assembly, and the Secretary-General?[14] How will it co-ordinate the policies and activities of the World Bank, the IMF, GATT/WTO, the Economic and Social Council (ECOSOC), the UN Environment Programme (UNEP), the UN Development Programme (UNDP) and other relevant UN agencies and programmes?

The Commission on Global Governance (1995) recognized (p342) that the *'time is now ripe – indeed overdue – to build a global forum that can provide leadership in economic, social and environmental fields. This should be more representative than the Group of Seven or the Bretton Woods institutions, and more effective than the present UN system.'*

The Commission recommended the establishment of an Economic Security Council (ESC) that would meet at high political level. Its tasks would be to:

- continuously assess the overall state of the world economy and the interaction between major policy areas;
- provide a long-term strategic policy framework in order to promote stable, balanced, and sustainable development;

- secure consistency between the policy goals of the major international organizations, particularly the Bretton Woods bodies and the WTO; and
- give political leadership and promote consensus on international economic issues.

The Commission recommended that the ESC should be established as a distinct body within the UN family, structured like the Security Council, though not with identical membership and independent of it. There are no doubt alternatives to an Economic Security Council as the way forward. But strengthening and re-orientating the economic policy-making capacity of the UN system should be an important goal for European policy-makers concerned with sustainable development.

5.4. SHORT-TERM AND LONG-TERM PRIORITIES

We now live in a one-world community, a global village. We have a globalized economy. Very few of the world's six billion people would be able to escape entirely from it into isolated local community economies, even if they wanted to. But accepting that it is here to stay is not to accept that it should continue to operate as it does now.

If we look to the longer term, we should expect historians in the 22nd century to be astonished that people living now were conditioned to believe that the only way to gain a satisfactory livelihood was by competing with people on the far side of the world to produce and sell products most of which were not strictly necessary for a decent quality of life. But in the shorter term, for policy makers today and in the immediate future, the question of how to compete effectively in a competitive global economy will continue to be high on the agenda.

There need not be an irreconcilable conflict here between the short term and the long term. Reducing the economic costs arising from high unemployment, environmental degradation, environmentally caused ill-health, inefficient use of resources, and local economic decline, will make an urgently needed contribution now to national and European economic competitiveness. This is one reason why the new economics agenda will continue to attract mainstream interest, and why policy makers will give increasing attention to self-reliant local socio-economic development. But, in the course of the next few decades, the spread of self-reliant local development around the world could help to bring about a reversal of global economic priorities, shifting the focus to local community wellbeing – economic, social and environmental – with transnational corporations and other global economic players taking on a supporting role.

In that context, what was said earlier about NGOs and citizens' movements bears repetition. They are playing an increasingly important part in the evolution of global economic policies and institutions. Many are closely linked with the growth of local community initiatives, local environmental initiatives, and third-sector socio-economic initiatives and community enterprises of all kinds, all over the world. They are almost all committed to people-centred development, as opposed to development that is business-centred or state-centred. They will be an increasingly important force for government policy makers to take into account.

5.5. SUMMARY OF POLICY IMPLICATIONS

European policy makers (at national and European levels) should aim to:

- show that Europeans are committed to reorienting our own way of life towards sustainable development;
- ensure that our own national and European activities in the spheres of international trade, investment and aid contribute to sustainable development elsewhere in the world; and

- participate effectively with the rest of the international community in evolving new global policies in support of sustainable and equitable development.

National governments and the European Commission should regularly review their policies on export promotion, outward investment, aid and technology transfer, with the aim of ensuring that they contribute to sustainable, not unsustainable, development in recipient countries. They should look for ways to help their own countries' consumers and investors to support 'fair trade'.

In cooperation with their own NGOs and international NGOs, they should actively help to shape the further evolution of institutions of global economic governance and global policies for sustainable development. In particular, this will mean:

- evolving a regulatory framework for international trade which, while discouraging protectionism, will encourage self-reliant, conserving development;
- cancelling unrepayable debts of poorest Third World countries;
- developing a system of global taxation based on charging nations for the use they make of common global resources – the revenue from which will be used partly to provide all nations with a per capita 'citizen's income' (in place of much of today's development aid to Third World countries), and partly to fund the UN system and its operations;
- developing a more effective system of management for the international monetary and financial system, possibly including the introduction of a global currency; and
- restructuring the institutions of global economic governance, to co-ordinate the policies and activities of the World Bank, IMF and WTO more closely with those of other parts of the UN system, under the supervision of a new world economic council more widely representative than the existing Group of Seven.

Notes

1 Keynes, J.M. (1933) 'National Self-Sufficiency' in Moggridge D (ed.) *The Collected Writings of J.M. Keynes*, Macmillan, London.

2 The WTO came into existence as the successor organization to GATT, 'to implement the Uruguay Round, provide a forum for negotiation, administer the new mechanisms for dispute settlement and trade policy review, and co-ordinate with the IMF and World Bank for greater coherence in global policy making' (Commission on Global Governance (1995), p168).

3 The peoples of the South will also be offered help to limit the growth of their populations. But if the North overemphasizes the need to limit population growth in the South, the South will simply respond that it is more urgent for the North to reduce consumption and pollution – and also to reduce its population, since every child born in the North will consume and pollute up to sixty times as much as a child born in the South.

4 Wuppertal 1995 – see Annex C, section 1.

5 WWF 1997.

6 Where a framework of regulation, taxation and public expenditure does exist, as in a national economy, it constitutes a different reason why a totally 'free' market is impossible. The characteristics of the framework help to determine the price structure of the economy in one way or another. See 3.2.2.

7 To make rather a different point, some have suggested the *reductio-ad-absurdum conclusion* that, if capital is allowed to flow freely across international boundaries, labour should be free to do the same, and all immigration controls throughout the world should be dismantled!

8 Tradable pollution permits issued by the UN might, in principle, be an alternative to taxes and charges. But the administrative difficulties would be formidable, apart from other possible objections (see Chapter 3).

9 This is known as a Tobin tax after James Tobin, the Nobel prize-winning economist who proposed it. It could serve a number of different purposes: to raise revenue; to discourage currency speculation; and, by building a cost threshold for imports and exports, to encourage national (or, where a local currency existed, local) economic self-reliance.

10 These included a proposal (from CAMDUN – *Conference on a More Democratic United Nations*) for a Second Assembly, to which the peoples of the world would elect their own representatives, in addition to the existing General Assembly in which governments are represented by government appointees; and a proposal (from Jakob von Uexkull of the Right Livelihood Foundation) for a People's Council for Sustainability as a third 'leg' to represent people at the UN, alongside the 'legs' based on wealth (the Bretton Woods institutions) and nation states (other UN institutions).

11 Their paper, *A World In Need Of Leadership: Tomorrow's United Nations*, was published in 1990 by the Dag Hammarskjold Foundation, Ovre Slottsgatan 2, S-753 10 Uppsala, Sweden.

12 *Common Responsibility In The 1990s: The Stockholm Initiative on Global Security and Governance*, (1991), from the Prime Minister's Office, S-103 Stockholm, Sweden.

13 As mentioned in 1.2, a significant landmark in the development of the new economics movement was the The Other Economic Summit meeting held in London in 1984, to draw attention to the inadequacy of the Group of Seven as a world economic council and the irrelevance of its annual summit agendas to the real concerns of people all over the world.

14 These questions were discussed in *World Economic Summits: The Role of Representative Groups in the Governance of the World Economy* (1989), from the World Institute for Development Economics Research (WIDER) UN University, Annankatu 42 C, SF-00100 Helsinki, Finland.

Chapter 6

From growth to sustainable development: some further questions

'The certainties of one age are the problems of the next.'

R.H. Tawney (1922)[1]

Conventional economic policies and theories have given pride of place to increasing money incomes – for example, as an indicator of economic progress (GDP based on National Income Accounts), as a criterion for assessing the merits of policy options (cost/benefit analysis), and as a basis for rising tax revenues. The new economics proposes new ways of measuring economic progress, new ways of assessing policy options, and (as outlined in Chapter 3) a new basis for taxation.

Thus the shift to sustainable development is likely to involve a shift of emphasis away from income growth. Questions arise about:

- economic measurement, accounting, calculation and analysis;
- the implications of developing an economy in which saving costs becomes as important, or more important, than generating income;
- possible links between new models of sustainable economy and new models in science.

6.1. MEASUREMENT AND ACCOUNTING

It is always important to measure characteristics that are significant for the purpose in hand. As the purpose changes, what is significant to measure also changes. As shifting to sustainable development becomes the goal, economic performance and prospects must be measured in different ways from the conventional ones.

The new ways of measuring now needed include new indicators and new accounting and auditing procedures. They are needed at global, national, local, corporate and household/personal levels. A great amount of work on their development is already in hand, including work within the European Union and elsewhere to develop environmental accounts linked with national accounts.

At national level, the principal conventional indicator of economic growth, Gross Domestic Product (GDP), which aggregates all kinds of income whether they add to wellbeing or not, was not originally designed to reflect wellbeing, and does not do so. A Sustainable Economic Welfare Index (ISEW) adjusts GDP by subtracting incomes from activities that diminish wellbeing or clearly do not add to it – such as depletion of non-renewable resources. An ISEW for the UK just published by the New Economics Foundation shows that although GDP per capita has increased by about a third since 1979, sustainable economic welfare has fallen by a fifth during the same period.[2]

There are two main ways of dealing with the inadequacy of GDP as a policy goal and as a measure of national economic performance.

One is to continue to use a single aggregate money figure but to adjust it, as the ISEW does. There are, however, two serious problems.

- First, it is not an entirely straightforward matter to compile an aggregate of incomes as a basis for the present National Income Accounts. It is much less straightforward to calculate the social and environmental costs and benefits to be subtracted from them or added to them in an adjusted ISEW. Notional estimates have to be made, and value judgements, implicit if not explicit, are involved.

- Second, no money-based index can provide an objective measure of welfare, equally valid for everyone. The same thing is worth more money to some people than to others. The same amount of money is worth more to poorer people than to richer people. A single money-based index cannot show who receives what benefits and who has to bear what costs. This is always an important policy question.

The other approach is to supplement GDP with a range of social and environmental indicators (and other economic and financial indicators), directly reflecting specific aspects of quality of life that are of concern, such as life expectancy, morbidity, air and water quality, fossil fuel emissions, and traffic congestion. Each indicator may be used separately to assess how it is trending. Or a set of indicators may be converted into a single index as a measure of quality of life, sustainability, or human development (or as an 'ecological footprint'). Using particular indicators will provide information for many policy decisions. But a single composite index (like the UNDP's Human Development Index) can usefully compare the quality of life or sustainability of different countries or different localities, and show how their present quality of life compares with what it was.

As time passes and the demand for sustainable policies becomes more pressing, the importance of real-life indicators and indices as guides to national policy aims, national policy targets, and measures of national policy achievement, will grow. For so long as tax revenues remain largely tied to incomes and profits and value added, National Income statistics will retain a functional importance for economic policy makers. But (see Chapter 3) the burden of tax is likely to shift away from incomes towards the use of energy and other resources.

At local level, the development of local sustainability indicators is proceeding as an aspect of Local Agenda 21. (The question of their relationship to a local equivalent of GDP does not arise, because local equivalents of GDP do not exist.) The New Economics Foundation and others are helping local government authorities and other local groups to develop local sustainability indicators through a participatory process of democratic consultation.

At corporate level, the objective of maximizing profits for shareholders has paralleled the public policy objective of GDP growth. Social and environmental accounting and accreditation (section 2.7) will place new constraints on profit maximization, even if it does not displace it as the principal corporate goal. The restructuring of taxation (Chapter 3) will give fresh impetus to corporate cost saving.

At household/personal level, the development of sustainability indicators and ways of measuring a household's or person's ecological footprint has still a long way to go. But organizations like Global Action Plan (See Appendix B, 4.4.2) are helping their members to assess the sustainability of their lifestyles. It is too early to say how this may eventually affect people's assessment of their income needs.

6.2. BEYOND COST/BENEFIT ANALYSIS

Cost/benefit analysis has a more limited contribution to make to policy decisions than conventional economics has appeared to suggest.

A calculation of costs and benefits can usefully clarify some of the factors relevant to a particular issue. But, just as no money-based index can provide an objective measure of welfare, so an objective calculation of 'true' costs and benefits cannot be made. It is a conceptual impossibility, for the following reasons.

- All the relevant costs and benefits extending into the distant future can never be identified, calculated and agreed.
- One person's money-measured cost is necessarily another's benefit. People (and organizations) are the only entities that pay and receive money. If someone pays costs, someone else receives income.
- The prevailing structure of prices and costs is influenced one way or another by the framework of government regulation, taxation and public spending existing at the time. Economic policy making is about how the framework (and therefore the prevailing structure of costs and prices) should be changed.
- The same thing is worth more to some people than to others.
- The same amount of money is worth more to some (poorer) people than to other (richer) people.

The upshot is that *'cost/benefit analysis, which assumes that a society has a single objective function on which all citizens agree, and a single metric by which all goods and bads can be measured, cannot be reconciled with pluralistic democracy'*.[3] It cannot relieve policy makers of responsibility for exercising political judgement.

Cost/benefit analysis can only make a subordinate contribution to policy decisions. Even in that role, more pluralistic and transparent deliberative procedures need to be developed to supplement it.[4]

6.3. THE MEANING OF ECONOMIC EFFICIENCY

Efficiency reflects a relationship between significant inputs and significant outputs. The greater the output in relation to the input, the greater the efficiency. The meaning of efficiency applicable in any particular case depends on what inputs and what outputs are regarded as significant – what inputs is it most important to reduce, and what outputs is it most important to increase? The shift to sustainable development changes the answers to that question.

135

For example, conventional economics has assumed (see 2.1) that an efficient farm produces a high ratio between the profits earned (output) and the number of workers employed (input). Ratios between the calorific value of food outputs and the calorific value of farm inputs, or between the amount of food produced (output) and the area of land farmed (input), have not been regarded as significant. Nor have the externalized costs of water, air and land pollution, soil erosion, impact on human health, destruction of wildlife and wildlife habitats, and rural unemployment. That has to change.

In general, conventional economics has assumed that efficiency involves the replacement of informal (unpaid) by formal (paid) economic activities; the replacement of labour by capital; and the maximization of profits, productivity, and economic growth. The new economics recognizes:

- that efficiency refers to the best (or, at least, a satisfactory) way of achieving the purpose(s) in hand;
- that the purposes of sustainable people–centred economic activity will be different from those of conventional economic activity;
- that before the efficiency of any particular activity can be established, the purpose(s) of the activity must be defined;
- that the activity will usually have a number of different purposes that have to be balanced, which usually in practice cannot be treated as one objective function to be maximized with the others as constraints; and
- that efficiency cannot usually be assessed on the basis of a ratio between one most significant output and one most significant input.

What the concept of efficiency means in the new context of sustainable development is a question that applies to every field of policy. Policy makers may find it helpful to consider it for their particular field.

6.4. INTERNALIZE COSTS OR PAY 'RENT'?

The normal rationale for the Polluter Pays Principle, and more generally for environmental and resource taxes, has been that those who impose costs on other people or on society or on future generations should be required to bear those costs themselves: costs now externalized (borne publicly) should be internalized (borne privately). Another equally relevant principle has hitherto figured less prominently in discussion of environmental taxes and charges. This is that people should pay 'rent' to society for the natural and societal resources they use: benefits now internalized (enjoyed privately) should be externalized (enjoyed publicly).

Do these two principles amount to much the same thing? Are there any significant theoretical or practical differences between the principle of internalized costs and the principle of rent?

The calculation of costs to be internalized is fraught with the same difficulties as those summarized at 6.2 above. In cases where the rights to use natural and societal resources are marketable, such as a plot of land or an airport landing slot, the calculation of rental values is more straightforward. But even here there are questions to be clarified. For example, today's market values will not take account of the interests of future generations. Nor will equating 'rent' with 'earnings from exploiting a natural resource in excess of costs of production and a reasonable rate of return on fixed capital' necessarily do so either.[5] It depends on what is assumed to be reasonable!

However, 'rental' payments could be appropriate for the following.

- land use,
- energy use,
- use of the environment's capacity to absorb pollution and waste,

- use of space, e.g. traffic congestion, aircraft landing/take off slots, space satellites,
- use of water, e.g. extraction, traffic (canals, rivers, oceans),
- use of the electro-magnetic spectrum,
- use of genetic resources, and
- use of the money system (related to 'seignorage', the revenue accruing to monarchs from issuing currency).

There is an international, as well as a national and local, dimension in every case.

As a general rule, the arguments in favour of using the principle of paying for benefits enjoyed, as a basis for raising public revenue from ecotaxes and related taxes, may well turn out to be stronger than the arguments for using the principle of internalizing externalized costs. The key question is which problems on the environmental agenda could not be adequately addressed by the general principle of requiring people to pay for the use of land and natural resources.[6] This is a point that needs to be explored further.

In either case, it will not be possible to calculate accurately or objectively what the 'correct' payments should be. That does not matter, any more than that it is not possible now to calculate objectively what the correct rates of income tax or value added tax should be. Having accepted that people should pay for the benefits they enjoy from the use of common resources (or for the costs they impose on other people), policy makers should be content to take a rough and ready approach to the level of the taxes and charges to be raised.

The level favoured by individual policy makers and policy-making groups will, of course, depend on their stance on questions of political principle. Should all citizens of a society and all people in the world, including future generations, enjoy – as nearly as practicable – an equal share in the value of common resources which they themselves have played no part in helping to create? Or are there other principles of equal weight – e.g.

that people who now enjoy more than an equal share should continue to do so, that society should be geared to allow successful people to take more than an equal share, or that society as a whole gains from having a privileged elite in this respect? The issues underlying these questions go back at least to Thomas Hobbes and John Locke. They are for political philosophers as much as for economists.

6.5. TOWARDS A COST-SAVING ECONOMY?

It is apparent that many of the changes involved in the shift to sustainable development will involve a shift of financial emphasis towards saving expenditure and reducing costs, in contrast with the emphasis on increasing incomes and revenues that has been typical of conventional economic progress. Some of these changes have been mentioned already in this section. But there are others.

Reductions in employment taxes and income taxes are likely to reduce the cost of employing people. As it then becomes economic for employers to provide paid work for more people, the costs arising from high unemployment may fall too. The Citizen's Income may result in more people choosing to do useful unpaid work, leading to some reduction of demand for marketed goods and public services. Higher energy and resource taxes, though raising short-term costs, may encourage reductions in energy and resource costs over the longer term. Reduced damage to health and the environment from energy-intensive, polluting activities may result in reduced health costs and environmental clean-up costs. The site-value tax on land may tend to reduce land costs for land users. The Citizen's Income and the land and energy taxes will cost less to administer than the social security benefits and taxes they replace. This will reduce the administrative costs of government and the costs of tax administration now borne by businesses and individual taxpayers. Because one person's costs are another person's income, these reductions in costs will mean corresponding reductions in income for the people and organizations to whom the costs have previously been paid. This will put those people and organizations, in their turn, under pressure to reduce their costs.[7]

Nonetheless, a drive to save costs may well be a feature of the transition to sustainability that must take place over the next half-century or more. It will reflect the need to internalize costs now externalized, in order to get them saved. It will reflect the need to prevent ecological and social damage before it occurs, in order to avoid continually rising remedial costs of dealing with the results of environmental destruction, ill health, poverty, ignorance and crime.

If – as an aspect of a cost-reducing economy – total public expenditure gradually falls, that will be in tune with a shift to a tax structure in which taxes on energy and resources and pollution (which tend to reduce their own base) play a central part. As the tax revenue from them falls, the costs of government which that revenue has to support will also be falling. Those will include the cost of the Citizen's Income, the level of which will fall as costs of living fall.

Conventional economics would tend to regard this prospect of a downward multiplier effect, a general shift of emphasis away from generating more income towards incurring less expenditure, as unconditionally disastrous, regardless of whether it helps to improve the quality of people's lives or is a necessary aspect of the shift to sustainable development. But the practical and theoretical issues it raises need to be carefully explored nonetheless.

The financial consequences could be very serious. If cash flows fall, capital asset values that depend on them are also likely to fall. Practical contingency planning will be required to minimize the damaging effects of an uncontrolled downward spiral. Theoretical studies comparing the differences between economic systems where the driving imperative is to reduce costs and those where it is to increase income could produce useful policy insights.

6.6. NEW MODELS IN ECONOMICS AND SCIENCE

The emergence of the worldwide movement for a new economics, concerned with the transformation of today's conventional patterns of economic activity and thought into a new economics of person, society and planet, is not an isolated phenomenon. Post-modern developments in science have also been taking place. How will new economics influence and be influenced by new science? To what extent will the new economics and the new science share the same conceptual foundations? Might study of these questions be relevant to the shift to sustainable development?

Newtonian physics no longer provides the dominant model for science. Systems theory, the study of interactive processes, the morphogenetic and developmental theories of the biological sciences, and mathematical theories about chaos and turbulence, are more typical of today's scientific frontiers. It is beginning to be accepted that scientists are not value-free observers; they cannot be altogether detached from the world that they observe. Scientists belong to the particular society in which they happen to live, and the questions they ask are greatly influenced by social, economic and cultural factors.

Increasing attention is now being given to experiential types of knowledge and understanding, acquired not by external observation but by direct participation in the processes about which knowledge and understanding are sought. In the economic and social spheres, this takes the form of participatory research. This cannot be divorced from ethical and political issues. The new knowledge it brings cannot be dissociated from action, nor its epistemology from its ethics.

Crucial aspects of contemporary science, including medicine, are about:

- the role of information and codes and decision rules in systems of every kind;

141

- patterns of energy flow and energy use;
- processes of structural change;
- interactive relations between systems and subsystems;
- factors determining whether a system is efficient, well-functioning, or inefficient, malfunctioning and unhealthy;
- relations between the measurable and the unmeasurable, quantity and quality, matter and mind; and
- the role of ethics in science.

All these have their analogues in economic processes. Economic life is increasingly concerned with information. The advent of electronic money reminds us that money is information (see 4.2.2). It provides information about people's entitlements and obligations – a scoring system for regulating economic activities, transactions and relationships. Looked at another way, money is energy. Flows and stocks of money reflect and determine flows and stocks of economic energy. Laws, regulations, management procedures and corporate cultures embody decision rules that help to shape economic behaviour. Altering them in the hope of reshaping economic behaviour has been compared with the alteration of genetic codes in biotechnology.

In economics, increasing attention is now being given to relations between – on the one hand – the unquantified, informal, non-monetized sphere of economic activity in which goods and services are directly used by the producer and the producer's family and friends, and – on the other hand – the quantified, formal, monetized sphere in which goods and services are produced for exchange. This parallels the growing attention being given to relations between complementary and allopathic medicine. 'Barefoot' economists, who participate in the economic activity they are studying, have something in common with physicists whose observations affect the behaviour of the particles they are observing.[8] The dual mechanism of cancer growth in biological systems – the formation of cancer cells accompanied by the weakening of the immune system – has analogues, such

142

as the spread of crime, in the economic and social sphere. An approach to agriculture based on pesticides, and to health based on allopathic medicine, is analogous to an approach to crime that emphasizes police and courts and prisons.

Can analogies like those be explored analytically and scientifically in depth, or are they just metaphorical parallels? Are the same or similar structural and mathematical patterns found, on the one hand in particular physical and biological functions and malfunctions, and on the other in particular economic and social functions and malfunctions? Do the links between information and energy provide a basis for modelling comparable developments in biological and economic systems? Might it be possible to show, for example, that similar patterns arise in the development of certain cancers as, say, in the overdevelopment of Third World cities, or the overdevelopment of financial flows and financial institutions in the global and national economy? Could this provide insights of practical value in both the economic and the medical sphere?

Questions like these fall well outside the boundaries of conventional economic research and policy analysis. But that is not to say that their possible relevance to sustainable development should be ignored. There is a task here that someone should be asked to undertake.

6.7. SUMMARY OF POLICY IMPLICATIONS

The shift to sustainability calls for new ways of measuring economic achievement, of accounting for it, of assessing policy options, and of redefining economic efficiency in every field of policy.

A key question arising from the development of environmental and resource taxation is whether the principle underlying it should be seen as the internalization of costs now externalized, or as payment for the use of common resources. This is not just a theoretical question. The answer to it will provide practical guidance for policies on the further introduction of environmental and resource taxes.

143

A widespread shift of emphasis from raising incomes to reducing costs could be part of the shift to sustainability. This could have serious effects for the financial system. Practical contingency planning is needed. Theoretical study of how a conventional economic system driven by rising incomes and the money-must-grow principle (see 4.1) differs from a sustainable economic system is also needed.

The relationship between the changing conceptual foundations of science and the future of the discipline of economics will be relevant to sustainable development. This is a topic that needs research.

Notes

1 R.H. Tawney, *Religion and the Rise of Capitalism*, Penguin, 1938, p275.
2 *More Isn't Always Better*, April 1997. The New Economics Foundation is an important source of expertise on new indicators and new accounting and audit methods.
3 John Adams, in *Cost-Benefit Analysis: Part of the Problem, not the Solution*, a paper for a seminar at Green College Centre for Environmental Policy and Understanding, March 1995.
4 Michael Jacobs, *After Cost-Benefit Analysis: Deliberative Institutions and Public Decision Making*, a paper for the above seminar.
5 UK Office of National Statistics, *Pilot Environmental Accounts*, August 1996, p45.
6 This question was suggested in a personal communication from Fred Harrison.
7 It is true, of course, that reducing labour costs has been a key feature of 'developed' economies for a long time. But it cannot be argued from that that it would not matter, if – across every other aspect of economic activity too – the drive to save costs becomes more powerful than the drive to generate higher incomes and revenues. Saving labour costs on a large scale does not, in fact, save them. It merely transforms them into rising unemployment costs.
8 Manfred Max-Neef (1982), *From The Outside Looking In: Experiences in 'Barefoot Economics'*, Dag Hammarskjold Foundation, Uppsala, Sweden.

Annex A

BACKGROUND AND TERMS OF REFERENCE

In 1997 the Forward Studies Unit asked if I would undertake a study for the European Commission on the policy implications of an alternative economic approach to sustainable development.

I was aware that sustainable development and new economics were the subject of a rapidly growing number of publications, conferences and projects in Europe and elsewhere, and that an increasing number of institutes, foundations and NGOs were now actively involved. I knew of several relevant projects sponsored by various Directorates-General in the European Commission. It would be pointless, even if I were able to do it, to try to summarize all this work and provide a comprehensive bibliography and resource list for it. And it would be impossible to go into the detailed practical implications in each field of policy to which the new economics applies.

What I would hope to do, drawing primarily on developments in the English-speaking world, would be to provide the European Commission with a sketch map of the new economics approach, drawing out key principles and policy implications, showing interrelationships between its various elements, and giving illustrative examples of published material and sources of information about them.

In due course, the assignment was formally agreed with the Institute for Prospective Technological Studies (IPTS) on behalf of the Forward Studies Unit as the ultimate client, with the following terms of reference.

1. Provide a value-added review of recent alternative-economic-paradigms work as it pertains to sustainability, with a particular emphasis on the practical/policy implications of such alternative views.
2. The work should be complementary to the sustainable development report by IPTS (1995), titled 'Sustainable Development: Towards a Synthesis', which had a more mainstream perspective. Research should cover more recent work (last two to three years) to deal with views posterior to the IPTS report.
3. The resulting work should specifically deal with issues of definitions of sustainability, the practical repercussions of alternative definitions/conceptions, the implications for environmental accounting, the role of substitution across forms of natural and man-made capital, the role(s) of technology, long-term and short-term concerns/repercussions, and the use and suitability of various policy instruments.
4. The emphasis should be on the practical implications aspects of various approaches, starting with the synthesis report by IPTS mentioned above.

THE SYNTHESIS REPORT BY IPTS

It was emphasized by the Forward Studies Unit that this review was to be complementary to the IPTS Report in the sense that it would take a different approach. It would not be expected to provide an updating of that report, nor to focus closely on the particular issues covered by it. However, the IPTS Report clearly calls for comment.

For theoretical economists, in the new economics movement as elsewhere, the IPTS Report is clearly of very considerable interest and value as 'a distilled version of the salient topics in current [academic economic] thinking on sustainable development' (page 3). There can be no dispute about that.

Two particularly important points of agreement between the IPTS Report and the new economics are the Report's recognition (page 27) of:

- the political dimension of sustainable development, and
- the difficulty of separating the environmental and social aspects of sustainable development.

The new economics approach strongly emphasizes that every aspect of the shift to sustainable development inevitably raises political issues, and that sustainability must be defined to include economic, social and environmental sustainability – all three.

Of the more specific issues at 3 above, the new economics emphasizes:

- the importance of further development of *environmental (and social) accounting*;
- the need for *technologies* that are conserving for the environment and enabling (as opposed to dependency-creating) for people;
- the need to *dovetail short-term with long-term strategies*, and
- the key roles of taxation and public expenditure as *policy instruments*.

But, given their orientation towards action, many people involved in the new economics give lower priority to exploring:

- definitions of sustainability, and
- the scope for substituting man-made capital for natural capital.

They give higher priority to the evident and urgent need to shift towards a path of development that is more sustainable and less destructive of natural capital.

Next, there is a set of related assumptions in the IPTS Report with which many new economics thinkers and activists positively disagree:

- the assumption that, in principle, *objectively optimal economic decisions* can be discovered by analysis based on monetary values (throughout the IPTS Report);
- the assumption that *GDP growth is desirable* (pages 8 and 9) and zero growth undesirable (page 15); and
- the assumption of the need to *account for sustainability in terms of monetary values* (pages 9–11).

The new economics takes the view that:

- money does not, and conceptually could not, provide an *objective* measure of value;
- important and difficult economic policy decisions are essentially political decisions about who is to gain and who is to suffer from possible courses of action;
- conventional measurement of economic growth – whether positive, zero, or negative – does not reflect sustainability or welfare, and is becoming increasingly misleading as a surrogate measurement for them; and
- accounting for sustainability and measuring progress towards it cannot rely on actual and notional monetary values; those must be supplemented or even replaced by non-monetary variables reflecting particular real-life aspects of sustainability and quality of life.

These points are more fully discussed in Chapter 6 of this book.

Finally, many people in the new economics movement, though not necessarily critical of the IPTS Report on its own terms, would probably not find it easy to draw practical policy conclusions from the analysis it presents.

Annex B

GROUPS AND ORGANIZATIONS

This is an illustrative list of some organizations involved in new economics. The list is not at all comprehensive. Entries appear under the section in which reference to them is first made or to which they are especially relevant. Most are relevant to other sections as well.

Introduction

European Commission, Cellule de Prospective, rue de la Loi 200, B-1049 Brussels, Belgium (Marc Luyckx).

European Commission – Joint Research Centre, Institute for Prospective Technological Studies, World Trade Centre, Isla de la Cartuja s/n, Sevilla 41092, Spain (Dimitris Kyriakou).

Chapter 1: The new economics

The two following organizations offer a wide coverage of new economics.

New Economics Foundation, 1st Floor, Vine Court, 112–116 Whitechapel Road, London E1 1JE (Ed Mayo).

General coverage of new economics issues. Quarterly magazine. Current programmes include: community economic development; new economic indicators; social auditing and codes of conduct for business; value-based organizations; sustainable consumption; social entrepreneurs; and education for a new economics.

Sustainable Economy Unit, Forum for the Future, 227a City Road, London EC1V 1JT (Paul Ekins).

Identifies ten strategic issues: greening the national accounts; implementing ecological tax reform; harnessing trade to sustainable development; linking sustainability, work and the welfare state; restructuring transport; reforming support for agriculture; developing solar power and energy efficiency; promoting a green industrial strategy; strengthening the local economy as an aspect of Local Agenda 21; and promoting environmental investment.

British Government Panel on Sustainable Development, Floor 23, Portland House, Stag Place, London SW1E 5DF (Sir Crispin Tickell).

CAG Consultants, 262 Holloway Road, London N7 6NE (Roger Levett). Strategic Planning for Sustainable Development.

Friends of the Earth Europe, 29 rue Blanche, 1050 Brussels.

Friends of the Earth London, 26–28 Underwood Street, London N1 7JQ (Duncan McLaren, Sustainable Development Unit).

Green Alliance, 49 Wellington Street, London WC2E 7BN (Stephen Tindale).

Green College Centre For Environmental Policy and Understanding, Oxford OX2 6HG (Sir Crispin Tickell).

Global Action Plan, 3rd Floor, 42 Kingsway, London WC2B 6EX (Trewin Restorick).

Institute of Noetic Sciences, 475 Gate Five Road, Suite 300, Sausalito, CA 94965, USA (Thomas J. Hurley).

People-Centred Development Forum, 14 E 17th Street, Suite 5, New York, NY 10003, USA (David Korten).

Real World Coalition, c/o Town and Country Planning Association, 17 Carlton House Terrace, London SW1Y 5AS.

Redefining Progress, 1 Kearny Street, 4th Floor, San Francisco, CA 94108, USA.

World Resources Institute, 1709 New York Avenue NW, Washington DC, 20006, USA.

Wuppertal Institute (for Climate, Environment and Energy), PO Box 100408, D-42004 Wuppertal, Germany (Ernst U. von Weizsacker).

WWF Europe, 36 Avenue de Tervuren B12, B-1040 Brussels (Tony Long).

Chapter 2: A common pattern

2.1. Farming and food

Agricultural Reform Group, Institute for European Environmental Policy, Dean Bradley House, 52 Horseferry Road, London SW1P 2AG (David Baldock).

SAFE (Sustainable Agriculture, Food and Environment) Alliance, 38 Ebury Street, London SW1W 0LU (Vicki Hird).

2.2. Travel and transport

Transport 2000, Walkden House, 10 Melton Street, London NW1 2EJ (Stephen Joseph).

2.3. Energy

Association for the Conservation of Energy, Westgate House, Prebend Street, London NW1 8PT (Andrew Warren).

International Institute for Energy Conservation (Europe), 1–2 Purley Place, London N1 1QA (Director: Stewart Boyle).

Rocky Mountain Institute, 1739 Snowmass Creek Road, Snowmass, CO 81654, USA (Amory Lovins).

2.4. Work, livelihoods and social cohesion

Europe 99, 21 Bd. de Grenelle, 75015 Paris (Valerie Peugeot).

Justice Office, Conference of Religious of Ireland (CORI), Tabor House, Milltown Park, Dublin 6 (Fr. Sean Healy). Ten-sector plan to ensure full citizenship for all.

2.5. Local development

Associacao IN LOCO, Apartado 603, 8000 Faro, Portugal (Alberto Melo).

European Network for Economic Self-Help and Local Development, Technical University of Berlin, Franklinstrasse 28/29, D-10587 Berlin, Germany (Karl Birkholzer).

151

Sustainable London Trust, 7 Chamberlain Street, London NW1
8XB (John Jopling).
Sustainable Gloucestershire,Vision 21, 16 Portland Street, Chelten-
ham, Glos GL52 2PB (Lindsey Colbourne).
URBED (Urban and Economic Development), 19 Store Street,
London WC1E 7DH (Nicholas Falk).

2.6. *Technology*

Intermediate Technology Development Group (ITDG), Myson
House, Railway Terrace, Rugby CV21 3HT, England.

2.7. *Business*

Sustainability Ltd, 49–53 Kensington High Street, London W8
5ED (John Elkington).
Centre for Social and Environmental Accounting Research
(CSEAR), University of Dundee, Dundee DD1 4HN, Scotland
(Rob Gray).
Centre for Tomorrow's Company, RSA, 8 John Adam Street,
London WC2N 6EZ.
Institute of Social and Ethical Accountability, 1st Floor, Vine
Court, 112–116 Whitechapel Road, London E1 1JE.
New Academy of Business, 3–4 Albion Place, Galena Road,
London W6 0LT.
World Business Academy, PO Box 191210, San Francisco,
California 94119, USA.

Chapter 3: Taxation and public spending

3.1.1. *Ecotax reform*

The following is in addition to organizations mentioned above,
and in Annex C 3.1.1:

Unitax Association, 50 New Road, Great Baddow, Chelmsford, Essex CM2 7QT, England (Owen Ephraim). *Developing software support for simulating the effects of shifting the tax burden to energy taxes and land tax.*

3.1.2. Site-value land taxation

Land Policy Council, 7 Kings Road, Teddington, Middlesex TW11 0QB, England (Fred Harrison). Important resource on Georgist taxation.

Henry George Foundation of Great Britain, 177 Vauxhall Bridge Road, London SW1V 1EU.

3.1.3. Citizen's Income

Basic Income European Network (BIEN), Philippe van Parijs, Université Catholique de Louvain, Chaire Houver, 3 Place Montesquieu, B-1348 Louvain-la-Neuve, Belgium.

Citizen's Income Research Group, St Philips Building, Sheffield Street, London WC2A 2EX (Rosalind Stevens-Strohmann).

CORI *(see above under Work, Livelihoods and Social Cohesion). Practical proposals for introducing a basic income in Ireland.*

Chapter 4: Money and finance

BankWatch, New Economics Foundation (see above).

Grameen Bank, Mirpur Two, Dhaka 1216, Bangladesh.

IFF (Institute for Financial Services and Consumer Protection), Burchardstrasse 22, D-20095 Hamburg, Germany (Udo Reifner).

INAISE (International Association of Investors in the Social Economy), Rue d'Arlon 40, B-1000 Brussels, Belgium (Viviane Vandemeulebroucke).

LETSlink, 61 Woodcock Road, Warminster, Wiltshire BA12 9DH, England (Liz Shephard).

Microcredit Summit, c/o RESULTS Educational Fund, 236 Mass Ave NE, Suite 300, Washington, DC 20002, USA (Sam Daley-Harris).

Triodos Bank, Brunel House, 11 The Promenade, Clifton, Bristol BS8 3NN (Glen Saunders).

UKSIF (UK Social Investment Forum), 318 Summer Lane, Birmingham B19 4RL (Pat Conaty).

Chapter 5: The global economy

Bread for the World Institute (World Bank Watchers and Development Bank Watchers), 1100 Wayne Ave, Suite 1000, Silver Spring, MD 20910, USA (Nancy Alexander).

Catholic Institute for International Relations (CIIR), Unit 3, Canonbury Yard, 190a New North Road, London N1 7BJ.

Christian Aid, PO Box 100, London SE1 7RT (Michael Taylor).

IIED (International Institute for Environment and Development), 3 Endsleigh Street, London WC1H 0DD (Nick Robins).

OXFAM, 274 Banbury Road, Oxford OX2 7DZ.

UNED-UK, c/o United Nations Association's Sustainable Development Unit, 3 Whitehall Court, London SW1A 2EL (Derek Osborn).

Chapter 6: From growth to sustainable development

See entries under Chapter 1 above.

Annex C

REFERENCES AND BIBLIOGRAPHY

This is an illustrative selection of books and publications relevant to the new economics. It is in no way comprehensive. Items are listed under the section of the book in which reference to them is first made or to which they are especially relevant. Many are relevant to other sections too. The number of web-sites on the World Wide Web on new economics topics is growing rapidly. They are not referenced here.

Introduction

Datta, A. (1997) *For a Quiet Revolution*, Papyrus, Calcutta.

Ecologist Magazine, (1972) *A Blueprint For Survival*, Penguin, Harmondsworth.

European Commission (1993) *Growth, Competitiveness, Employment: The Challenges and Ways Forward into the 21st Century*, Brussels.

Kyriakou, D. (1995) *Sustainable Development: Towards a Synthesis*, European Commission Institute for Prospective Technological Studies, Seville.

Meadows, D. et al (1972) *The Limits To Growth*, Pan Books, London.

Schumacher, E.F. (1973) *Small Is Beautiful: A Study of Economics As If People Mattered*, Blond & Briggs, London.

Ward, B. and Dubos, R. (1972) *Only One Earth: The Care and Maintenance of a Small Planet*, Penguin, Harmondsworth.

Chapter 1: The new economics

Brandt, B. (1995) *Whole Life Economics: Revaluing Daily Life*, New Society Publishers, Philadelphia.

British Government Panel on Sustainable Development (1995, 1996 and 1997) *First, Second and Third Reports*, Department of the Environment, London.

Buarque, C. (1993) *The End of Economics? Ethics and the Disorder of Progress*, Zed Books, London.

Daly, H. (ed.) (1973) *Toward A Steady State Economy*, Freeman, San Francisco.

Daly, H. (1996) *Beyond Growth*, Beacon Press, Boston.

Daly, H. and Cobb, J. (1989) *For the Common Good: Redirecting the Economy Towards Community, The Environment and a Sustainable Future*, Beacon Press, Boston.

Douthwaite, R. (1992), *The Growth Illusion*, Green Books, Devon.

Ekins, P. (ed.) (1986) *The Living Economy: A New Economics in the Making*, Routledge & Kegan Paul, London.

Ekins, P. et al (1992) *Wealth Beyond Measure*, Gaia Books, London.

Ekins, P. and Max Neef M. (1992) *Real-Life Economics*, Routledge, London.

General Consultative Forum to DG XI (1996-97), *Vision 2020: Scenarios for a Sustainable Europe*, Working Document. (Scenario 3: Transforming Communities is perhaps the nearest to the new economics vision.)

Harcourt, W. (1994) *Feminist Perspectives on Sustainable Development*, Zed Books, London.

Harman, W. (1976) *An Incomplete Guide to the Future*, Stanford Alumni, California.

Henderson, H. (1978) *Creating Alternative Futures: The End of Economics*, Berkley Publishing, New York.

Henderson, H. (1996) *Building a Win-Win World: Life Beyond Global Economic Warfare*, Berrett-Koehler, San Francisco.

Higgin, G. (1973) *Symptoms of Tomorrow*, Plume Press, London.

156

Higgins, R. (1978) *The Seventh Enemy: The Human Factor in the Global Crisis*, Hodder and Stoughton, London.

Hoogendijk, W. (1991) *The Economic Revolution: Towards a Sustainable Future by Freeing the Economy from Money-making*, Greenprint, London.

Jacobs, M. (1991) *The Green Economy*, Pluto Press, London.

Jacobs, M. (1996) *The Politics of the Real World*, Earthscan, London.

Latouche, S. (1993) *In The Wake Of The Affluent Society: An Exploration of Post-development*, Zed Books, London.

Mishan, E.J. (1967) *The Costs of Economic Growth*, Penguin, London.

New Economics Foundation (quarterly) *New Economics*, NEF, London.

Ormerod, P. (1994) *The Death Of Economics*, Faber, London.

Robertson, J. (1978, 1983) *The Same Alternative: A Choice of Futures*, Robertson, Oxfordshire.

Robertson J. (1990) *Future Wealth: A New Economics for the 21st Century*, Cassell, London.

Sachs, W. (1992) *The Development Dictionary: A Guide to Knowledge as Power*, Zed Books, London.

Seabrook, J. (1993) *Pioneers Of Change: Experiments in Creating a Human Society*, Zed Books, London.

Shiva, V. (1991) *The Violence of the Green Revolution*, Zed Books, London and Third World Network, Penang, Malaysia.

Spapens, P. and Vervoordeldonk, R. (1995) *Towards A Sustainable Europe*, Friends of the Earth Europe, Brussels. (This is a summary of a 244pp report from the Wuppertal Institute. 4-page recommendations from November 1995 Sustainable Europe Conference are also available.)

Sustainable Economy Unit (1996) *Programme For A Sustainable Economy*, Forum for The Future, London.

'Vision 2020' (1996) *Scenarios for a Sustainable Europe*, a Working Document for the General Consultative Forum to DG XI, Brussels.

von Weizsacker, EU (1994) *Earth Politics*, Zed Books, London.

von Weizsacker, EU, Lovins, A. and Lovins, H. (1997) *Factor Four: Doubling Wealth, Halving Resource Use*, Earthscan, London (forthcoming).

WWF Europe (1996) *EU Structural Funds – More Value for Money*, WWF Europe, Brussels.

Wuppertal Institute (1995) *Sustainable Germany: A Contribution to Sustainable Global Development*, Wuppertal Institute, Germany.

Chapter 2: A common pattern

2.1. Farming and food

Development (1996: 4) *Food Security and Development*, Society for International Development, Rome.

New Economics Foundation (January 1996) *Sustainable Agriculture: Economic Alternatives for Eastern Europe* (Vol. 3), NEF, London.

Paxton, A. (1994) *The Food Miles Report: The Dangers of Long Distance Food Transport*, SAFE Alliance, London.

SAFE Alliance/CIIR Briefing (November 1996) *The Fischler Reforms: Options for the CAP*, SAFE/CIIR, London.

Shiva, V. (1991) *The Violence of the Green Revolution*, Zed Books, London.

WWF Europe (1996) *New Objectives for the CAP: Article 39 of the Treaty of the European Union*, WWF European Policy Office, Brussels.

2.2. Travel and transport

Gleave, S.D. (1995) *Alternatives to Traffic Growth: The Role of Public Transport and the Future for Freight*, Transport 2000, London.

Royal Commission on Environmental Pollution (1994) *Transport and the Environment*, HMSO, London.

Tourism Concern, *Tourism in Focus*, magazine of Tourism Concern, London.

2.3. Energy

See relevant items under Chapter 1 and 3.1.1.

2.4. Work, livelihoods and social cohesion

Development (1996: 3) *Civil Society: The Third Sector in Action*, Society for International Development, Rome.

Hulbert, A. (1996) *Towards an Economy of Care and Compassion*, Occasional Paper No. 3, Ecumenical Association for Church and Society, Brussels.

Judge, A.J.N. (1996) *Sustainable Lifestyles and the Future of Work* (and other papers on Work), Union of International Associations, Brussels.

Justice Commission (1997) *Planning for Progress: Tackling Poverty, Unemployment and Exclusion*, Socio-Economic Review 1997, Conference on Religious of Ireland, Dublin.

Lerner, S. (1994) *The Future of Work in North America: Good Jobs, Bad Jobs, Beyond Jobs*, Futures, 26/2, Oxford.

Rifkin, J. (1995) *The End of Work*, Putnam, New York.

Robertson, J. (1985) *Future Work: Jobs, Self-Employment and Leisure after the Industrial Age*, Gower/Temple-Smith, Aldershot.

Robertson, J. (1995) *Electronics, Environment and Employment*, Futures, 27/5, Oxford.

2.5. Local development

Colbourne, L. (ed.) (1996) *Sustainable Gloucestershire*, Vision 21, Cheltenham.

Douthwaite, R. (1996) *Short Circuit: Strengthening Local Economies for Security in an Unstable World*, Green Books, Devon.

Girardet, H. (1992) *Cities: New Directions for Sustainable Urban Living*, Gaia Books, London.

Jopling J. and Girardet H. (1996) *Creating a Sustainable London*, Sustainable London Trust, London.

Morehouse, W. (ed.) (with Benello, C.G., Swann, R., Turnbull, S.) (1989) *Building Sustainable Communities: Tools and Concepts for Self-Reliant Economic Change*, Bootstrap Press, New York.

Pearce, J. (1993) *At the Heart of the Community Economy: Community enterprise in a changing world*, Gulbenkian Foundation, London.

Stott, M. et al (1996) three articles appraising local exchange trading systems in *Local Economy*, Vol. 11, No. 3, Local Economy Policy Unit, South Bank University, London.

Wackernagel, M. and Rees, W. (1996) *Our Ecological Footprint: Reducing Human Impact on the Earth*, New Society Publishers, Philadelphia.

2.6. Technology

Cooper, T. (1994) *Beyond Recycling: The Longer Life Option*, New Economics Foundation, London.

2.7. Business

Davis, J. (1991) *Greening Business: Managing for Sustainable Development*, Blackwell, Oxford.

Hawken, P. (1993) *The Ecology of Commerce: How Business Can Save the Planet*, Harper Collins, New York.

Korten, D.C. (1995) *When Corporations Rule the World*, Berrett-Koehler, San Francisco.

Schmidheiny, S. (1992) *Changing Course: A Global Business Perspective on Development and the Environment*, MIT Press, Cambridge, Mass.

Welford, R. and Starkey, R. (eds.) (1996) *Business and the Environment*, Earthscan, London.

2.9. Conclusion

Goyder, G. (1987) *The Just Company: A Blueprint for the Responsible Company* (republished by Adamantine Press, London, 1991).

Turnbull, S. (1995) *New Money Sources and Profit Motives – for democratising the wealth of nations*, The Company Directors Association of Australia.

Chapter 3: Taxation and public spending

3.1. A restructured tax system and a Citizen's Income

Kemball–Cook et al (1991) *The Green Budget*, Greenprint, London.
Mulgan, G. and Murray, R. (1993) *Reconnecting Taxation*, Demos, London.
Robertson, J. (1994) *Benefits and Taxes: A Radical Strategy*, New Economics Foundation, London.

3.1.1. Ecotax Reform

DIW, German Institute for Economic Research (1994) *Ecological Tax Reform Even If Germany Has To Go It Alone*, Economic Bulletin, Vol. 37, Gower, Aldershot.
Ekins, P. (1996) *Environmental Taxes and Charges: National Experiences and Plans*. Report of a European workshop, European Foundation for the Improvement of Living and Working Conditions, Dublin. (Papers by 15 participants are available in a separate volume.)
European Environment Agency (1996) *Environmental Taxes: Implementation and Environmental Effectiveness*, Environmental Issues Series No. 1, European Environment Agency, Copenhagen.
Friends of the Earth (1996) *Green Dividends: Why the Chancellor should invest in Ecotax Reform*, Friends of the Earth, London.
Norwegian Green Tax Commission (1996) *Policies for a Better Environment and High Employment*, Norwegian Government, Oslo.
O'Riordan, T. (ed.) (1997) *Ecotaxation*, Earthscan, London.
Repetto, R. et al (1992) *Green Fees: How a Tax Shift Can Work for the Environment and the Economy*, World Resources Institute, New York.

von Weizsacker, EU and Jesinghaus, J. (1992) *Ecological Tax Reform*, Zed Books, London.

3.1.2. Site-value land taxation

Banks, R. (1989) *Costing the Earth*, Shepheard-Walwyn, London.

Burgess, R. (1993) *Public Revenue Without Taxation*, Shepheard-Walwyn, London.

Gaffney, M. and Harrison F. (1994) *The Corruption of Economics*, Shepheard-Walwyn, London.

George, H. (1878) *Progress and Poverty*, Hogarth Press, London (condensed edition 1953).

Land and Liberty (quarterly magazine), Henry George Foundation of Great Britain, London.

Noyes, R. (ed.) (1991) *Now the Synthesis: Capitalism, Socialism and the New Social Contract*, Shepheard-Walwyn, London.

Ricardo, D. (1817) *The Principles of Political Economy and Taxation*, (Everyman Library edition, J.M. Dent, London 1911).

Tideman, N. (ed.) (1994) *Land and Taxation*, Shepheard-Walwyn, London.

3.1.3. Citizen's Income (or Basic Income)

Basic Income Newsletter (quarterly), Basic Income European Network.

Brittan, S. and Webb, S. (1990) *Beyond the Welfare State: An Examination of Basic Incomes in a Market Economy*, Aberdeen University Press.

Citizen's Income Bulletin (quarterly), Citizen's Income Research Group, London.

Clark, C. and Healy, J. (1997) *Pathways to a Basic Income*, Justice Commission, Conference of Religious of Ireland, Dublin.

Parker, H. (1991) *Basic Income and the Labour Market*, Citizen's Income Research Group, London.

Parker, H. (1993) *Citizen's Income and Women*, Citizen's Income Research Group, London.

Schutz, R. (1996) *The $30,000 Solution: A Guaranteed Annual Income for Every American*, Fithian Press, California.

van Parijs, P. (1992) *Arguing for Basic Income: Ethical Foundations for a Radical Reform*, Verso Press, London.

Chapter 4: Money and finance

Greenpeace Business (bi-monthly), Greenpeace, London.

Greco, T.H. (1994) *New Money for Healthy Communities*, Greco, Tucson, Arizona.

Hayek, F.A. (1978) *Denationalisation of Money*, Institute of Economic Affairs, London.

Hoogendijk, W. (with contributions by Binswanger, H.C.) (1995) *Money – From Master To Servant*, Promodeco, Utrecht (unpublished paper).

IFF (1996) *Bank Safety and Soundness* – The Bergamo Report, Conference Proceedings, Institut für Finanzdienstleistungen, Hamburg.

INAISE/UKSIF (1995) *Developing Social Wealth: Financing the Social Economy*. International Association of Investors in the Social Economy, Brussels, and UK Social Investment Forum, Birmingham.

Jacobs, J. (1984) *Cities and the Wealth of Nations: Principles of Economic Life*, Random House, New York.

Kennedy, M. (1995) *Interest and Inflation-Free Money: Creating an Exchange Medium that Works for Everybody and Protects the Earth*, New Society, Philadelphia.

Kurtzman, J. (1993) *The Death of Money: How the Electronic Economy has Destabilised the World's Markets and Created Financial Chaos*, Simon and Schuster, New York.

Lietaer, B.A. (1996) *The Future of Money*, unpublished draft.

Mayo, E. (ed.) (1993) *BankWatch*, New Economics Foundation, London.

New Economics Foundation (1996) *Money Matters: Taking Charge of our Money, our Values and our Lives*, resource list and annotated bibliography, NEF, London.

Mulgan, G. (1994) *Creating a Twin Economy*, article in The End of Unemployment: Bringing Work to Life, Demos Quarterly 2/94, London.

Solomon, L. (1996) *Rethinking our Centralised Monetary System: The Case for a System of Local Currencies*, Praeger, Connecticut.

Tomlinson, J. (1993) *Honest Money: A Challenge to Banking*, Helix Editions, Oxfordshire.

Walker, P. et al (1996) *LETS on low income*, New Economics Foundation, London.

Chapter 5: The global economy

Brown, M.B. (1993) *Fair Trade*, Zed Books, London.

Cleveland, H., Henderson, H. and Kaul I. (eds.) (1995) *The United Nations at Fifty: Policy and Financing Alternatives*, Special Issue of *Futures*, Vol. 27, No. 2, Butterworth-Heineman, Oxfordshire.

Commission on Global Governance (1995) *Our Global Neighbourhood*, Oxford University Press, Oxford.

Ekins, P. (1993) *Trading Off the Future*, New Economics Foundation, London.

Ekins, P. (1995) *Harnessing Trade to Sustainable Development*, Green College Centre for Environmental Policy and Understanding, Oxford.

Independent Commission on Population and Quality of Life (1996) *Caring for the Future*, Oxford University Press, Oxford.

Lang, T. and Hines, C. (1993) *The New Protectionism: Protecting the Future Against Free Trade*, Earthscan, London.

NEF/CIIR (1997) *Open Trading: options for effective monitoring of corporate codes of conduct*, New Economics Foundation and Catholic Institute for International Relations, London.

World Commission on Environment and Development (1987) *Our Common Future*, Oxford University Press, Oxford.

WWF Europe (1997) *A European Sustainable Development Initiative for EU Development Cooperation* (proposal for discussion), WWF European Policy Office, Brussels.

Chapter 6: From growth to sustainable development

Adams, J. (1995) *Cost-Benefit Analysis: Part of the Problem, not the Solution*, Green College Centre for Environmental Policy and Understanding, Oxford.

Max-Neef, M. (1982) *From the Outside Looking In: Experiences in 'Barefoot Economics'*, Dag Hammarskjold Foundation, Uppsala, Sweden.

New Economics Foundation for WWF (1995) *New Directions for Structural Funds: Indicators for Sustainable Development in Europe*, NEF, London.

New Economics Foundation (quarterly) Indicators Update, NEF, London.

New Economics Foundation (1997) *More Isn't Always Better* (a special briefing on growth and quality of life in the UK), NEF, London.

The Forward Studies Unit

The Forward Studies Unit was set up in 1989 as a department of the European Commission reporting direct to the President.

It consists of a multicultural, multidisciplinary team of some 15 people who are responsible for monitoring the forward march of European integration while identifying structural trends and long-term prospects.

The Commission decision setting up the Unit[1] gave it three tasks:

- to monitor and evaluate European integration to 1992 and beyond;
- to establish permanent relations with national bodies involved in forecasting;
- to work on specific briefs.

The Forward Studies Unit has, to date, produced wide-ranging reports on new issues which, as a result, have frequently found their way into the mainstream of the Commission's work, developing a house style which applies a research method designed to bring out the diversity of Europe *(shaping factors, shaping actors)*, developing an all-round and/or long-term view which makes it easier to secure consensus above and beyond particular national interests, keeping a watching brief on and an ear open to movements in Europe's societies by setting up links with research and forward studies institutions, and holding regular seminars on specific themes which are attended by prominent figures from the arts, the cultural sphere and universities and representatives of civil society, together with the President or a Member of the European Commission.

167

The futurological function has gradually developed outside the Unit, within several of the Commission's Directorates-General which are keen to adopt a strategic approach. The Unit serves as a point where all the various future-oriented think tanks inside the Commission can meet together.

For some years now, the need for a forecasting function having grown as the work of the European Union has become wider and more complex, the work programme for the Forward Studies Unit has been updated each year so that it can be reoriented to meet specific needs and towards maximum cooperation with all the Commission departments concerned.

Information about the Unit's current work is put out in the quarterly *Lettre des Carrefours* and on an Internet site:

http://europa.eu.int/comm/cdp/index_en.htm

Note

1 Minutes of the 955th meeting of the Commission, 8 March 1989.